Reflections on Higher Education

Reflections on Higher Education

M.S. Sodha
R. Soni

KALPAZ

ISBN : 978-93-532-4005-9

First Published, 2019

Published by

Kalpaz Publications
C-30, Satyawati Nagar,
Delhi – 110052
Ph.: 011-47034999, 9811692060
www.kalpazpublications.com
E-mail: kalpaz@hotmail.com

Printed at: G. Print Process, Delhi

Dedicated to our Parents

Late Shrimati Saraswati Devi Sodha

Late Shri Jai Dutt Sodha

and

Shri Satya Prakash Soni

Shrimati Uma Soni

Contents

Preface

The academic activities in Education have been mostly confined to Higher Secondary Education. It is only recently that professors and others have started taking interest in pedagogical aspects of higher education. The governance of Higher Education is considered to be the exclusive concern of the government; the sacred book is the University Act, considered to be outside the domain of all, who are governed by it. The apparent concern is about government and government aided institutions. The private universities/colleges are governed by the same system with a little tinkering. The fact that the budget for higher education is shrinking while the costs are going up has made us to take an integrated view of higher education, covering all aspects of higher education viz. academics, finance, administration, governance, internationalization etc. In academics there is widespread concern about employability/placement and finance of private institutions. There is also a debate about the desirability of excellence in education at the cost of higher fees; this is all the more relevant in the context of some excellent private institutions with high fees. Of course some seats can be reserved to be filled by merit at comparable fees in government institution. Many innovative steps can be taken but none without enhancement in fees. There is a mood to deny excellence to few, who can afford it without doing anything about the rest. It is hard to understand this logic, when faced with gross inequities in consumer consumption. Why is one allowed to own a Mercedes when others cannot have a Nano? Of course we are given a justification, based on economics. In our case nobody takes into account the value enhancement of a youth by excellence in education.

This book presents a discussion of various aspects of higher education, with emphasis on CHANGE. The reflections are concerned with employability, discipline, financing of excellence, education for profit, internationalization, coaching institutions, emotional intelligence etc. we will consider our effort worthwhile if it encourages free thinking and CHANGE.

Rashmi Soni
M S Sodha

Acknowledgment

The authors are grateful to their institutions for support and invigorating environment. We have benefitted a lot by our interaction with intellectuals in Education and related fields. We would particularly like to mention late Professor B.K. Passi as a scholar and a source of inspiration. Our interaction with scholars at the University has extended our vision and refined our ideas. Special mention should be made of Prof. M.Varma, Prof. U.C. Vashishtha, Prof. Amita Bajpai, Prof. A.K. Sengupta, Prof. M. Muzammil, Prof. K.C. Pandey and Prof. P.K. Sahoo.

It would not have been possible without the benevolent umbrella provided by Prof. S.P. Singh, Vice Chancellor, Lucknow University and Prof. S.D. Sharma, Principal, J.N.P.G College. Acknowledgement will not be complete without mention of all round support of our families and friends.

Rashmi Soni
M S Sodha

Reflection - 1

A Vision of Higher Education: Empowering Youth through Emotional Intelligence

Introduction

> "We cannot always build the future for our youth, but we can build our youth for the future."—Franklin D. Roosevelt, Former President, U.S.A.

East or West, North or South, youth everywhere, is in a state of restlessness and revolt. It was so in the past and it shall be so in future as well, howsoever glamorous and glittering the social fabric might become, and howsoever secure and stable they might feel under the new indulgence. The young have never rested on their past laurels; nor have they felt contented with their present possibilities. The chords of their impulses, instincts and intuitions are always vocal and vibrant. No doubt, the problems of youth in different parts of the world, under different socio-political systems, differ in form and content. But it is almost certain that the modern youth is up against problems, the like of which did not exist in the past. 'Youth in turmoil', 'Unrest among youth', 'Youth in revolt', 'Angry young man'—these epithets are not just literary coinage, but a vociferous voice of protest of vast segments of population that have seen and suffered the all-round erosion of values and ruining of their dreams.

Having been influenced by the philosophies of 'individualism' and 'existentialism', the urban youth is in a state of defiance against the old order, whether that order derives from the elderly generation or the powers that be. If they find themselves in a state of alienation or hostility in the present set-up, the fault lies as much with their socio-economic environment as with the education system. Deprived of the opportunity to develop intellectually, many suffer from the problem of subjective isolation and self-estrangement. Among red-tapism and bureaucratic control over the strings of both private and public sectors, the cream of the country finds itself uncared and un-solicited for. It is under these trying and turbulent circumstances that the best brains of the country start draining out. Those who succeed in finding jobs or some means of subsistence in India do not find life easy. A host of problems keep staring them in their faces like inadequate housing, transport and sewerage, poor medical and recreational facilities, neurotic noise pollution, shortages, dust, smoke, crimes, ever-expanding slums and what not.[1]

The leadership's failure to inspire the youth with their ideal thinking and action has made the Indian youth into either cynics or snobs, unable to cope with the day to day problems and predicaments. One of the big failures of the Indian models of development has been the inability to realize that we are dealing with a very different kind of society, comprising many linguistic and ethnic groups craving for recognition of their rights to preserve their ethnic and linguistic entity. The cult of Hippism, drug addiction, violence, aimless murders, etc. proves beyond doubt that mere material prosperity is not the end of all problems. The psychologists and psychiatrists point to the widespread enigma of neurosis-clam-mental sickness most prevalent among the youth.

We are witnessing a phenomenal advancement in technology over the last three decades, and our citizens are experiencing remarkable social and cultural change. This drastic change has generated psychological and social dislocations among many people. Moreover, technology has influenced the way we think about life in general and interpersonal human relations in particular. Television in particular has gone far beyond the mandate to assist the family and the school in providing visual aid to education of the young. It has taken on itself to appeal to the destructive and disintegrative instincts, to provoke greed, unlimited self-gratification, and lack of moral restraint in its young audience. If these tendencies are not kept in check by concern for the well-being of others, as taught by religion or otherwise, it could lead to a self-serving, ego-centered population.

The Indian Youth and Modern Education

The poem, "where the mind is without fear and the head is held high" represented Rabindranath Tagore's dream of how the new and awakened India should be; most importantly, the youth who would be advantaged to see the free, sovereign and independent India should be motivated and empowered. After many years of his passing away, has India lived up to his dream? As a country, India has come a long way; we are a free country in terms of the political rights we enjoy as citizens. However, in today's India, there is a persisting fear among the youth- the fear of competition. Even a six-year-old child who is supposed to be at the peak of fearlessness and cheerfulness worries about exams and cut-offs. Come exams and hundreds of students surrender their youthful enthusiasm to the fear of examinations, the insecurity of falling below the cut-off and, at times, sink into depression leading to a fatal end viz. suicide.

Suicide was the leading cause of death among youngsters aged 10-24 in the country, with 62,960 such deaths reported in 2013, according to the findings of the Lancet Commission on Adolescent Health and Well-being. The Commission studied three age groups viz. 10-14, 15-19 and 20-24 to find that in India, suicides were the leading cause of death in the second and third age groups and the seventh cause of death in the youngest age group (3,594 deaths). In absolute numbers, in 2013, 3,594 adolescents in the 10-14 age group killed themselves in India, 23,748 did so in the 15-19 age group and 35,618 in the 20-24 age group. According to Census 2011, there are 364.66 million youngsters in the 10-24 age groups, making up 30.11 per cent of the country's total population.[2]

"Adolescents today face new challenges, including rising levels of obesity, mental health disorders and high unemployment," Dr Vikram Patel, professor of International Mental Health at London School of Hygiene and Tropical Medicine, UK, and among the expert researchers of the Lancet report, told The Indian Express.

Every hour, one student commits suicide in India, according to 2015 data (the latest available) from the National Crime Records Bureau (NCRB). In 2015, the number of student suicides stood at 8,934. In the five years leading to 2015, 39,775 students killed themselves. The number of attempted suicides, many unreported, is likely to be much higher. In 2015, Maharashtra reported most student suicides of any state viz.1,230 of 8,934 (14%) nationwide, followed by Tamil Nadu (955) and Chhattisgarh (625). Maharashtra and Tamil Nadu are among India's most advanced states, and their high rate of suicides could reflect the pressures of economic growth.

Conversations with counsellors revealed that young people find it difficult to cope with failure in examinations and careers and neither families nor other social institutions offer adequate support or solace. Professional help is difficult to find because India endures an 87% shortage of mental-health professionals. The situation is exacerbated by low public spending on mental health — India spends less than Bangladesh on mental-health services. Family background, it would appear, has an important role in determining how young people cope with despair.

Students from "happy" families suffer from less depression, according to an October 2016 study conducted among Indian university students. Shaibya Saldanha, co-Founder of Enfold India, an NGO which works with children and adolescents, concurs with this reasoning." The popular perception is that failing exams or inability to cope with academics is the primary reason for student suicides," Saldanha told India Spend in an email interview. "This is rooted in a sense of helplessness or extreme frustration."

Student suicides are becoming increasingly common in Kota, Rajasthan, considered the capital of India's shadow education system. Its many commercial coaching centers, that guarantee success in professional entrance exams, pressure students into striving for unrealistic goals. Unable to cope with failure and anxious about letting their family down, a growing number of Kota students opt to end their lives. The 2016 study further found that students who studied social science and humanities, performed poorly in academics, or came from disadvantaged families reported higher rates of depression. Universities in India still lack counselling centers, where trained counsellors and psychologists can assist students at the onset of emotional and mental problems so they do not spiral into full-fledged clinical depression and lead to suicide.[3]

Close to 800 000 people die due to suicide every year, this is one person every 40 seconds. Many more attempt suicide. Suicide occurs throughout the lifespan and is the second leading cause of death among 15-29 year olds globally. Suicide is a global phenomenon; in fact, 78% of suicides occurred in low- and middle-income countries in 2015. Suicide accounted for 1.4% of all deaths worldwide, making it the 17th leading cause of death in 2015.[4] According to the National Crime Records Bureau (NCRB), nearly 1, 35,445 people took their lives in the past year. This figure of NCRB is based on police records. Since attempt to suicide is an offence in the country and stigma is attached to it, therefore many people prefer not to report such cases. Of the total cases of suicide, nearly 35 per cent were recorded in age group of 15-29 years. Meanwhile, the Lancet study pegs suicidal deaths in the same age group at 46 percent of the total. A comparison of the number of suicides in states with high literacy rates with those with low literacy rates reveals that the states with high literacy (top ten states) contribute 33 per cent to suicidal deaths. However, these states make up for not more than 21 per cent of India's population. While the states with poor literacy rates (below ten states) contribute roughly the same to the deaths, that is, 33.2 per cent, they account for a whopping 53 percent of the country's population. **Does this discrepancy make a case in point that the rise in literacy and the reach of modern education lead to increased levels of anxiety, depression and suicide among the youth, probably by unrealistic expectations?**

The society is increasingly becoming **achievement-based**. As a result, individuals are not appreciated for what they are and for their unique capabilities. They are judged based on the dominant perception of success prevailing in the society that values jobs and money. Humanistic psychologist like Carl Rogers and Abraham Maslow believe that everyone is inherently good and has equal potential for self-actualization. As a matter of fact, very often, as the Dalai Lama also says, "human nature is inherently good and loving". Since we are social beings, it is important for us to be accepted, appreciated and loved by others without any condition in order to realize our unique talents. But our society, parents, and we ourselves, impose what may be called conditions of worth on our children in order to be loved, accepted and recognized for their worth. This leads to denial and rejection of the real self within the child since conditions of worth do not allow an individual to fully understand and explore his/her likes or dislikes. This distorts the real self and may result in neurosis, depression and suicide.

The modern education system is oriented to gaining skills such as reading, writing, convergent thinking and numerical aptitude. It is aimed at increasing productivity rather than encouraging wisdom, confidence, warm-heartedness and life-dealing skills. Modern education has been over-emphasized in its role to remove the disadvantages that exist at individual, familial and society levels. After attaining this type of education, good scores, degrees and exposure to media bombardment, there is an increase in expectations, aspirations and unrealistic ambitions. Consequently, unfulfilled aspirations and expectations lead many youth either to adopt unethical means to achieve the aspiration or to frustration and depression. While chasing our modern elusive dreams we have forgotten as parents and teachers to prepare our children and youths in life skills and to become emotionally strong. There is a lack of value system or norms that can guide the actions of the youth trapped in a situation of unlimited aspirations, which exceed the opportunities and means available to fulfill them. The youth of today does not have the moral guidance to be able to pursue the right course when faced with a moral dilemma.

The present education system especially the higher education system needs to be over-hauled. Presently, the exams, marks and percentage do not test a student's abilities, skills, emotional intelligence and aptitude. Therefore it is high time we develop a scientific standard of gauging the students. The syllabus and texts taught in our schools and colleges must be drastically altered so that it helps improve our life skills or aid adjustment in society. According to a report by *Aspiring Minds*,[5] an employability solutions company, a significant number of graduates in India, nearly 47 per cent, was found unemployable in every sector. This brings us to the point that, in the near future, the percentage may not be relevant to get a job—in fact; one may be gauged on the basis of one's divergent thinking skills, emotional intelligence and team spirit.

Right now, in the name of education, a vicious cycle is creating and maintaining inequality, defeating the very purpose of education. There is need for re-structuring of the education system, so as to minimize competition and rivalry and thereby reduce feelings of marginalization and exclusion among low achievers. Also, there is need for reform of the curriculum so as to include universally desirable values and training of our youth in emotional intelligent skills that are necessary for producing well rounded, balanced, sensitized and useful citizens.

Need to cultivate Empathy in Youth

The day's headlines are a roll call of violent acts that make no sense. In our personal lives, the fallout of the neglect of our emotional selves is evident in many ways, including child abuse, poor parenting skills, escalating rates of violence among children, and teen suicides. Social pressures encourage us to disconnect from our emotional selves, and when we do, our repertoire of emotional responses gets severely limited. The emotional resources we bring to a challenge are depleted resulting in behavior that is antisocial and self-destructive.

Is the world going mad? No, say psychologists, we are simply losing the ability to empathize. Throughout the world, teachers, sociologists, policymakers and parents are discovering that empathy may be the single most important quality that must be nurtured in order to give peace a fighting chance. As the world struggles with violence the challenge is to reinstate and reaffirm values of tolerance, cooperation and respect. It is becoming increasingly evident that the ability to identify with others, and hence to respond appropriately to them, is crucial. It's a lesson that humans are continually challenged to re-learn.

The concept of empathy has been around for a long while. Most of the ancient religious systems such as Christianity, Buddhism, and Hinduism are imbued with it. But empathy and mastery of emotions have in general, been neglected by rationalism and the "hard" sciences, which have become such powerful forces in modern society. Education programs increasingly focus on powers of reasoning, cognitive ability, and rational thought to the exclusion of emotional literacy. The former have been seen as measures of intelligence and indicators of a person's potential for success. Feelings and emotions have been devalued, their display considered a sign of weakness and lack of control. This single-minded pursuit of cognitive intelligence is one of the greatest ironies of our times. As science and technology have made the world into a vast global village, human beings find themselves ill-equipped to succeed because they lack the abilities and skills that such a world without boundaries requires. To thrive in today's world depends on the ability to work cooperatively with strangers, to be tolerant, to respect and appreciate differences, and to be able to resolve conflicts in a constructive manner.

So if emotional literacy skills are developed at the same time one learns the traditional mathematical and literacy skills, there is a good chance our youths will turn out to be caring and compassionate adults who are good at managing relationships. Because they are in tune with their emotions and can be appropriately responsive to others', they will be good at creative problem solving and great team workers. Furthermore, developing empathy in early childhood is correlated to development of a strong set of personal ethics.

We all are emotional beings, with our thinking shaped by the good and bad experiences we encounter in our lives. With time, some of us become extremely emotional, while some become tough nuts, and some fail to reciprocate the feelings of others. Emotionally weak individuals find it tough to manage their thoughts; they have difficulty in taking negative feedback, and also tend to get upset at the slightest provocation. However, there are some people smarter in handling relationships, or a complex situation than others. They are not deeply emotional, but are considerate while dealing with people. Such people know what to speak and when to speak, when to keep quiet and be patient. They have a gut feeling and at any given moment they do, for them and others, what they think is right. Such people have a good emotional quotient (EQ), (a measure of emotional intelligence, just as IQ measures intelligence) its importance of which is growing with each passing day, surpassing even the highly valued intelligence quotient (IQ).

With the ever-increasing pressures at work, within the community, and at home, the ability of individuals to deal with the daily environmental demands and pressures is getting even more critical. Cognitive intelligence (IQ) accounts for up to 25% of the variance in professional success and job performance (Hunter & Hunter.[6] Social and emotional abilities are four times more important than IQ in determining success (Sternberg.[7] In 1990, Salovey and Mayer[8] coined the term "emotional intelligence" (EI) and based their work on the non-cognitive aspects of intelligence. These authors defined emotional intelligence as "a form of social intelligence that involves the ability to monitor one's own and others' thinking and action."

In any educational set up students in higher education interact within their communities and they face many emotional challenges. The 21st century students are often referred as Generation "Y". Generation Y is exposed to a lot of emotional challenges which requires higher educators to address or correct some of the behaviour in order to boost academic performance. Students in higher education are taught specific courses and there is a gap in terms of soft skills module such as emotional intelligence. Therefore it is imperative to introduce an emotional intelligence module to close the gap between academic subjects and the soft skill subjects. The more the students learn about reducing high emotions the more they perform better in their academic subjects. The skills for emotional intelligence may be developed throughout someone's life as they are part of lifelong learning and form the foundation for a balanced lifestyle.[9]

Understanding Emotions and Emotional Intelligence

The value of emotional understanding has only recently been recognized, since the parents and teachers have become increasingly concerned about children's social and emotional development. Emotional understanding is a key factor in children's emotional development and functioning. By serving as a link between the input of emotional stimuli and the consequent emotional expression or behavior, emotional understanding may serve as a mediating cognitive structure. Emotional understanding is also vital to human performance and the management of successful learning organizations. Even though the primary attention of education is academic performance, there is simply too much convincing evidence that schools and colleges should not and cannot neglect the development of emotional intelligence skills and other personal and social factors. Emerging trends necessitate new studies and applied research on the contributions of the emotional mind and the emotional domain of learning. Building healthy and productive students requires the active and intentional development of emotional intelligence skills and competencies as a normal and integral part of the process of education. To achieve this balanced perspective, the student development model of learning is reviewed and discussed. Many student development researchers and leaders have emphasized human development and affective learning as an essential component of the higher education experience.

"Emotional Intelligence (EI) describes the ability, capacity, skill or, in the case of the trait EI model, a self-perceived ability, to identify, asses, and manage the emotions of oneself, of others, and of groups." The term, 'emotional intelligence', literally means having wise emotions, which have the understanding of time and space. This means that one will exhibit one's emotions when the moment is right, which is why this behavior has been deemed as emotional intelligence at work.

According to Bar-On,[10] emotional intelligence is "an array of non-cognitive capabilities, competencies, and skills that influence one's ability to succeed in coping with environmental demands and pressures". Broadly defined, emotional intelligence "addresses the emotional, personal, social, and survival dimensions of intelligence". Emotional intelligence and emotional skills develop over time, change throughout life, and relate to one's potential for performance, are process-oriented, and can be improved through training. Dr. Reuven Bar-On developed the EQ-i: Bar-On Emotional Quotient Inventory, which measures 5 components and 15 subcomponents. These include:

- Intrapersonal- assertiveness, self-regard, self-actualization, independence, and emotional self-awareness
- Interpersonal-interpersonal relationships, social responsibility, and empathy
- Adaptability-problem solving, reality testing, and flexibility
- Stress Management-impulse control and stress tolerance
- General Mood-happiness and optimism

Their ability tests focus on, in particular, whether emotional intelligence can be grown and developed, although they accept that some people are born with higher levels of emotional intelligence than others. Their view is based on a belief that:

- Human beings are emotional animals and their emotions play a critical part in learning and in life.
- Being able to monitor our own and others' feelings and emotions, to discriminate among them and to use this information to guide our thinking is, perhaps, the most important life skill.
- Some people are innately more emotionally intelligent than others. However people can develop emotional intelligence, particularly at critical periods including infancy and teenage years.
- Emotional intelligence is a very complex area and, although our understanding is growing, there is still a great deal we do not understand.
- As yet, there is no universally recognized method of measuring emotional intelligence accurately, or demonstrating that it can be developed.
- Schools can help to teach young people how to develop their emotional intelligence. Classrooms also need to be emotionally secure places for both teachers and learners.

Although many definitions exist, the basic ideas are the same. Emotionally intelligent people are aware of their emotions and the emotions of others. They use that information to guide their thinking and actions.

Emotional Intelligence: A Higher Education Perspective

Understanding the crucial role which emotional competence plays in individual, group, and organizational success, its implication for education is clear i.e. we should be helping young people master these competencies as essential life skills. Efforts are being made to some extent to provide social and emotional learning (SEL) to students at school level but when it comes to preparing young people in the essential emotional intelligence skills that matter most for their success in the workplace, for piloting their careers, and for leadership, we face a serious gap. These programs cover the early school years but not higher education. Only a scattered handful of pioneering courses on social and emotional learning exist at the college or professional level. And yet the data showing the crucial role EI skills play in career success make a compelling case for re-envisioning higher education in order to give these capabilities their place in a well-rounded curriculum.

Emotional knowledge, skills, and intelligence hold a major key to improving education, helping students, teachers, faculty, student development and professionals attain higher degrees of achievement, career success, leadership, and personal well-being. There are many important issues and challenges facing education at the public school and higher education levels. While academic achievement and scholastic performance have been the primary thrust of recent reform efforts, other equally important issues have taken center stage in education. Physical safety, healthy emotional development, standards of excellence and equalitarianism, a global economy and world perspective, changing workforce demands and the nature of work, multi-cultural and diversity issues, retention through graduation, and personal/career needs of students and educators are just a few examples. These important issues require a different and more balanced perspective of accountability and quality standards to include emotional learning and the affective domain.

Academic and cognitive development is the primary and chief goal of schools, colleges, and universities. However, it may prove disastrous if the emotional and affective domain is neglected as an important and necessary role for schools and communities. A blending of academic (cognitive), behavioral (action), and affective (emotional) dimensions are needed to address the complex issues facing education. To meet the issues and challenges of education, especially higher education, there is a need to develop responsible and emotionally healthy students and teachers. Emotional skill development and personal responsibility need to be embraced and in effect just as it is with the academic and behavioral dimensions.

A widely reported national study by the American College Test organization on the topic of drop-outs in the freshman year of college revealed that academic ability (cognitive domain) was not the major factor. The primary reasons for dropping out were not academic but personal factors (emotional domain) such as loneliness, lack of purpose, and feelings of inadequacy. While academic development is the primary purpose of education, there is a wealth of information and experience that confirm the importance and impact of emotional intelligence skills and competencies. Extensive reviews of studies at schools and organizational levels indicate that emotional intelligence skills are essential to achievement, leadership, and personal health (Goleman.).[11]

In studying the world's best educational practices, Dryden and Vos[12] reported that personal and emotional development is at the very center of these programs. Their findings indicate that the emotional intelligence skills of self-esteem and personal confidence are essential to all learning. They declare that education that fails to address these factors (i.e. personal/emotional domain) will fail in its other tasks as well (Dryden and Vos, 1994). Leading educators have identified and emphasized the importance of a healthy school, college and university climate for student learning and achievement (Goodlad, 1983; McQuary).[13] Emotional intelligence skills and competencies are key to creating and maintaining a healthy and productive educational climate.

A college education may exhibit having leadership and career limiting if healthy emotional development is not viewed as important and necessary role in the entire college experience. To achieve the educational aspirations of the 21st century and to transform India through higher education, there is an increasing need to develop healthy, responsible, and productive students, teachers, faculty, staff, and administrators in all academic disciplines. Accountability needs to be embraced and in effect in academic, behavior, and emotional development. A number of leading researchers have concluded that emotional intelligence and related non-traditional measures of intelligence and human performance are as predictive (if not more so) of success as IQ tests and other standardized measures of scholastic ability and achievement (Salovey and Mayer;[14] Goleman, 1995, 1997; Dryden and Vos, 1994).

Interdisciplinary research clearly connects emotional intelligence and emotional skills to achievement, career success, personal health, well-being, and leadership. This line of research carries a crystal clear message for colleges and universities who strive to develop their students to the fullest. Fundamental beliefs and core values of student development in higher education should include the following:

- recognition of the preeminence of the academic mission of the university
- respect for the integrity and well-being of each student
- commitment to actively building a healthy and safe learning environment
- equality and fairness in serving all students
- a celebration of diversity

These beliefs and values are consistent with the academic goals of higher education. They need to be embraced with institutional commitment and accountability. Colleges and universities are expected to document how academic and student development programs lead to and result in student achievement, retention, career enhancement, and leadership development. A balanced system of accountability and commitment is needed. Student development programs, utilizing an education and research-based model of emotional intelligence competencies and skills, are needed to demonstrate this institutional commitment to accountability.

A college or university is viewed as a place where students grow through their involvement in meaningful relationships. Students' benefits from relationships that (1) make them feel valued, (2) contribute to positive self-worth, (3) create a healthy, productive learning community, and (4) form a personal sense of belonging. Healthy relationships are important to the academic, behavioral, emotional growth and development of students. Emotional knowledge, skills, and competencies are essential to the student development and values of appreciating individuation and community. The affective or emotional learning domain is central to student development. Experiential and self-directed learning activities need to be systematic and accountable. Colleges and universities need to be able to demonstrate and show faculty, students, and the entire academic community how courses, programs, services, and resources make a difference in professional and personal development. Student development programs are positioned to meet this type of institutional accountability.

Emotional intelligence skills are vital to human performance and the management of successful learning organizations. Even though the primary attention of education is academic performance, there is simply much convincing evidence that schools and colleges should not and cannot neglect the development of emotional intelligence skills and other personal and social factors. Emerging trends necessitate new studies and applied research on the contributions of the emotional mind and the emotional domain of learning. Building healthy and productive students requires the active and intentional development of emotional intelligence skills and competencies as a normal and integral part of the process of education. Many student development researchers and leaders have emphasized human development and affective learning as an essential component of the higher education experience.

For the past several decades higher education researchers have been advocating for institutional reform that places the learner at the center of a community of learners who are all engaged in a shared processes of human enlightenment. The implications very strongly suggest that learning is a process of interconnectivity that involves not just the rational intellect but the emotive and relational ones also. These research findings bring forth serious challenges to the current paradigm that rests on the theory that learning is best facilitated by isolating students from other students and teachers from students in sterile and separate disciplines where cross fertilization of thoughts and ideas are kept to a minimum. This evidence seems to suggest that many of the commonly accepted higher education practices and institutional structures may very well inhibit rather than facilitate the processes of learning.

The most important goal for every institution of higher education is academic development. However, in today's diversified society, students need much more to lead healthy and productive lives concerning academic, career and personal goals. Therefore, it is crucial for institutions of higher education to develop academic advising and student learning models that embodies both the academic (cognitive) and emotional (affective) development of students. Students with a strong academic and emotional foundation will model and demonstrate behaviors that are conducive to goal attainment and overall success in life. Consequently, leaders in student development must engage in applied institutional research to begin to develop and improve models for student retention and performance. This research is vital for students and higher education personnel to study and to model continuous program improvement and effective leadership.

Empowerment in Higher Education through Emotional Intelligence

The role of teachers in the development of emotional intelligence skill in students especially at the tertiary education (i.e. faculties of education and colleges of education) cannot be over-emphasized. Teachers should first acquire a skill to exploit the advantages of each dimension of students' emotional intelligence. Teachers should have knowledge of emotional intelligence so that they can help to develop the emotional intelligence amongst their students. Students should be taught the strategy to handle the problem of emotion and the ways to cooperate with others. It is when the students are able to control their emotion that they will be able to concentrate on their studies and profit credibility from the opportunities, the education offers.

Teachers equipped with adequate emotional intelligence skills would be able to generate a pleasurable classroom by having a dynamic group discussion with the students. Through this students would be able to identify the feelings of their mates and get the feedback based on their reaction i.e. they will develop the feeling of empathy. Such teachers would be able to apply several strategies to reduce the incidences of cultism, substance abuse, examination malpractices and poor academic performance prevalent in the higher tertiary education. By this strategy, teachers will be able to reduce the negative effect of students' anxiety in each learning process by constructing acceptable and pleasurable conditions that give psychological support to the students and empower them to lead a quality life.

Of significance to note is that the study towards the aspect of emotional intelligence is still very new; education researchers and others are hoped to be very inspired to give their attention to the study of emotional intelligence as it is relevant to the citizens' social and educational environment. The experts in educational psychology are called upon to consider and redesign the educational psychology curriculum that involves the issue of emotional intelligence. Emotional intelligence may be considered as a unit course in the psychology of development or Developmental Psychology courses that are offered in faculties of education and colleges of education.

Indeed, there is a merit in challenging the perception of what institutions can do for employers by making the correlation between the environment and style of learning in higher education and the positive impacts on developing emotional intelligence just as it happens in corporate and industries. However, universities are facing strong competition from an employer's in-house solutions for the development of talent, as well as private sector providers. Higher education institutions have untapped potential to lead with their own strategy, one that orients around developing the emotional intelligence of the individual through their life. Arguably, institutions must also work with schools and further education, prior to higher education, in order to begin the development of emotional intelligence. Furthermore, universities and colleges need context for their learning interventions and, therefore, should be forming partnerships with employers as early as possible in an individual's life.

When higher education institutions can articulate their learning environment in the context of developing emotional intelligence, they have the potential to provide a differentiated proposition to employers and establish a new dynamics of partnership. This is already (maybe) happening, but more can and should be done to benefit employers, employees and their leadership and management; so we continue to search for opportunities to collaborate and prepare the leaders of today and tomorrow for a changing world.

Higher Education literature indicates recent applications of emotional intelligence especially self-regard and how they can improve communication effectiveness. Self-regard plays an important role in emotional intelligence. Self-regard is individuals' perception of themselves. The self-concept can be an agent and motivates individuals to take on an action. Individuals with high self-regard tend to have higher emotional intelligence and this action lead to improvement in communication effectiveness. The goal of introducing instruction in emotional intelligence with communication effectiveness is to expose managers and administrators to a framework that describes specific competencies needed for educational administration. People with high self-regard are likely to have good communication, and will probably be successful in anything they decide to do .On the other hand people with low self-regard are likely to have a hard time in communication with others.

One area where emotional intelligence comes into play in the higher education organization is in providing feedback to employees. Too often critiques come across as personal attacks and employees play out the same scenarios they use in their families at the workplace. The scenarios become dysfunctional when applied to the workplace. Sarcasms, angry voices, and blanket criticisms only serve to destroy motivation. Employees feel they are being treated as children and may act out in ways that are not productive. Instead, Goleman suggests, as do most management texts, that positive coaching includes concentrating on behaviors and not the person, offering solutions, and being empathetic while discussing difficult issues with employees. For the employee receiving criticism, the challenge is to see the criticism as information that can be used to improve performance. Individuals with high emotional intelligence scores are better able to place the criticism in context and not see it as a personal attack, regardless of how the conversation is approached by the supervisor.

After understanding how important is Emotional Intelligence for the empowerment of our youth today and what role can Higher Education play to build emotional intelligence in them, the time has come to ponder sincerely and discuss and finalize the modus operandi about how to inculcate this important concept at various levels of Education. We need to discuss the blueprint of the syllabus that would be a guide for students and youth to imbibe different dimensions of Emotional Intelligence. The laboratories and workshops that need to be organized for the smooth running of this course deserve special attention.

Conclusion and Implications

The importance of promoting emotional education is questioned in the educational settings and the response of the educators to the importance of emotional education is mixed. Some claim that emotional education is "the missing piece"[15], yet some teachers may view it with skepticism as they believe that academic achievement is more important. However, as indicated by substantial literature, there is a direct link between the emotional status of the students and their performance in tests and examinations: increased anxiety and stress equates with poorer performance in these areas. Emotional stability indicates a wide array of expected and favorable outcomes. Emotional competence is seen as the knowledge about ourselves and others. It is also of the prime indicator of academic success[16] and this helps to have the capacity to solve problems adaptively, which is the crucial foundation for academic learning. Emotional competence of adolescents could be promoted by school-based intervention programs. The education can be carried out in diverse formats, such as classroom instruction, extra-curricular activities, or curricular-based programs. The emotional education programs aim at promoting skills "to listen or focus, to feel committed and responsible for work, to rein impulses, and to cope with upsetting events"[17]. This scaffolding provided by school-based programs becomes an important factor for developing students' emotional competence.

Notable countries belonging to the G8 (the richest countries club) such as the United States and the United Kingdom have begun to understand that being one of the eight most industrialized, richest and most influential countries on the planet does not guarantee that the citizens are satisfied with their lives or are happy. In the context of Malaysia, the aspect of emotional intelligence is primarily focused in the National Philosophy of Education. Spain finds itself at an excellent moment to make educational policies and investment similar to United States, United Kingdom and Malaysia. Each of these countries is pursuing emotional intelligence in their own way.

It is imperative to introduce a module on emotional intelligence in higher education. This module assists students in correcting their negative behaviour and attitudes. Therefore, if this module is implemented well the academic performance in higher education may improve.

In realizing the reality of emotional intelligence, the curriculum of education right from primary to tertiary education is being reviewed by considering the role of emotional intelligence. However, the efforts to implement the emotional intelligence in ensuring the accomplishment and the development of students' self should not be executed intellectually. The responsibility should not be borne only by the teachers, but the need of the hour is of a paradigm shift in the system of education together with professionalism of teacher education. The policy-maker of education should arrange the liberty and an approach as well as the firm support to ensure the balance of national education system with the aspect of emotional intelligence and intellectual intelligence.

In the academic world, the issue of emotional intelligence is still relatively new; therefore, many studies should be done before researchers establish clear and unambiguous relationships between the degree of emotional intelligence and success, both on personal and organizational levels. Because of its impact on today's organizational success, it is critical to implement effective EQ training into university and college curricula and system in order to prepare not only students but also teachers, and those in authorities for thriving corporate careers and successful personal relationships and of course at the end to be able to give quality education for which they have been established.

Leaders and managers need to understand their own emotions and recognize and understand the feelings of those around them. Leaders are more successful when they pay attention to their social interactions with others in the work place and the impact they as leaders have on those around them. It is also important for leaders to understand the impact that others' emotions have on them. When leaders are aware of the emotional side of the workplace along with the technical processes of getting tasks and goals accomplished, they are better able to create a working environment that encourages excellence. Managing our emotions means something quite different from stifling them. It means understanding them and then using that understanding to turn situations to our benefit.

Hopefully, most forward-thinking educators recognize the importance of emotional intelligence in higher education, not just for the empowerment of students, not just for empowering the teachers, but for the vitality and empowerment of the economy as a whole.

Specific References

1. https://www.youthkiawaaz.com/2011/03/problems-of-youth-in-turmoil/
2. http://indianexpress.com/article/india/india-news-india/suicide-leading-cause-of-death-among- indias-young-report-2792671/
3. https://www.hindustantimes.com/health-and-fitness/every-hour-one-student-commits-suicide-in- india/story-7UFFhSs6h1HNgrNO60FZ2O.html
4. http://www.who.int/mental_health/prevention/suicide/suicideprevent/en/
5. https://www.aspiringminds.com/sites/default/files/47_graduates_in_india_are_unemployable_for_ any_job_aspiring_minds_national_employability_report_graduates.pdf
6. Hunter, J. E., & Hunter, R. F. (1984). Validity and utility of alternative predictors of job performance. Psychological Bulletin, 96, 72–78.
7. Sternberg, R. J. (1997). *Successful intelligence*. New York: Plume
8. Salovey, P., & Mayer, J. (1990). Emotional intelligence. *Imagination, Cognition, and Personality, 9*(3), 185-211.
9. https://files.eric.ed.gov/fulltext/EJ1134442.pdf
10. Bar-On, R. (2002). *EQ-I: Bar-On emotional quotient inventory technical manual*. Toronto, Canada: Multi-Health Systems.
11. Goleman, Daniel (1995). Emotional Intelligence. New York, NY: Bantam Books.
12. Dryden, Gorden and Vos, Jeannete (1994). The Learning Revolution. Winnepeg, Canada: Skills of Learning Publications..
13. McQuary, John P. (1983). "Personal Skills Development in an Educational Setting". Corpus Christi, TX: A paper presented at the Personal Skills Mapping Conference..
14. Mayer, J. D., &Salovey, P. (1997). What is emotional intelligence? In P. Salovey, & D. Sluyter, Emotional development and emotional intelligence: educational implications. New York: Basic Books.
15. Elias MJ, Zins JE, Weissberg RP, et al. *Promoting Social and Emotional Learning: Guidelines for Educators*. Alexandria, Va, USA: Association for Supervision and Curriculum Development; 1997.

16. Zeidner M. *Hebrew Adaptation of the OCEANIC*. Haifa, Israel: Centre for Interdisciplinary Research on Emotions Press, University of Haifa; 2002.

17. Bar-On R. *The Emotional Intelligence Inventory (EQ-i): Technical Manual.* Toronto, Canada: Multi-Health Systems; 1997.

General References

Bar-On, R. (1988). The development of an operational concept of psychological wellbeing. Unpublished doctoral dissertation, Rhodes University, South Africa. Book, H. (2000, September). One big happy family: Emotional intelligence in the office. Ivey Business Journal, v65 i1, 44.

Bar-on (2006), *Emotional Quotient Inventory (EQ-i).* Technical Manual. Multi Health Systems. Toronto.

Cherniss, C., Goleman, D. (2001). *The Emotionally intelligent workplace: How to select for, measure, and improve emotional intelligence in individuals, groups, and organizations*. The Consortium for Research on Emotional Intelligence in Organizations.

Cote, S & Miners, C.T, (2006), "Emotional Intelligence, Cognitive Intelligence and Job Performance", *Administrative Science Quarterly* SKI), 1-28.

Goleman, D. (1995). *Emotional intelligence: Why it can matter more than IQ*. New York: Bantam.

Gardner, H. (1983). Goleman, D. (2000). Leadership that gets results. *Frames of mind.* New York: Basic Books Harvard Business Review, March-April.

Goleman, D. (1998). *Working with emotional intelligence*, New York: Bantam.

Goleman, D (1995*), Emotional Intelligence.* New York: Hantan Hooks.

Howard G & Salovey, P (2005), feeling Smart: The Science of emotional Intelligence. *American Scientist,* 93, 330-339.

Mayer, D., Salovey, P. (1993), 'The intelligence of Emotional Intelligence'. *Intelligence*, 17, 433-442.

Mayer, J. D Salovey, P. & Caruso, D. R. (2008), Emotional Intelligence. New Ability or Eclectic traits. *American Psychologists,* 63(6), 503-517.

Soni, R. (2013), *Higher Education: India and Abroad,* Atlantic Publishers: New Delhi.

Thorndike, R. K. (1920), *Intelligence and Its Uses,* Harper's Magazine 140, 227-335.

Trinidad, D. R. & Johnson, C. A. (2002), The Association between emotional Intelligence and early Adolescent Tobacco and Alcohol Use. *Personality & Individual Differences,* 32, 95-105.

Weisinger, H. (1998), Emotional intelligence at work. San Francisco: Jossey-Bass, 45-51.

Williams, W., Sternberg, R. (1988), Group intelligence: Why some groups are better than others. *Intelligence,* 12(4), 351-377.

Wikipedia *Emotional Intelligence.* The free encyclopedia

Reflection - 2

Higher Education for Profit

Introduction

In most parts of the world, higher education has long been understood overwhelmingly or even exclusively to be public. Today in most regions and countries, surging private higher education compels increased consideration of two separate sectors viz. public and private. Yet fast paced developments show that even dual-sector analysis is often too limited since for-profit higher education is on the rise. In the United States, where not-for-profit private higher education is extensive and often prestigious, the for-profit sector has grown dramatically in recent years, fueling discussion about markets and competition across all sectors of higher education. Meanwhile in some countries with traditional public dominance, for-profit higher education adds a fresh dimension to the global expansion of private higher education.[1]

The debate at the global level is related to the justification of providing higher education on profit basis, although what is profit and how the profit is used are the issues that are defined differently. If an institution imparting higher education which is charitable wants profit that is some money (remaining money) to be used for the expansion and improvement in quality, it should never be called profit making. Thus, even non-profit organizations may earn profit and reinvest the money in education. Purely profit oriented organizations are those that earn profit for being distributed among employees and the shareholders. This gives an opportunity to the government to tax these organizations. The money accruing to the government through taxes may in turn be spent for higher education through public institutions. Viewed thus, even profit making institutions are of social relevance.

It is reasonable, then, to speak of three higher education sectors viz. public, private non-profit and private for-profit. Globally, the private nonprofit sector is much more prevalent and important than the for-profit sector; the public sector is more prevalent and important than both private sectors together.

The present dismal scenario in India regarding the financing of higher education can however be a blessing in disguise, if it sets our mind free from stereotyped thinking to explore alternate and possibly better and more sustainable avenues for the creation of the required opportunities for meritorious and other students. The solution, so evolved can be feasible only if it can be implemented without putting any additional burden on the public exchequer. Until recently higher education was expected to be provided only by the government (public sector) but now the scenario is changing. Private provision is coming up fast. This is true not only in India but also globally. Traditional systems and traditional beliefs are giving way to a new order.

For-profit higher education may provide an answer. There appears to be an urgent demand for new elite institutions which can finance themselves and will meet the national and international requirement of highly competent manpower in critical areas and develop a unique culture of their own, which would be conducive to excellence. The private sector, if enabled and empowered can rise to the occasion, as the investment and initiative cannot come from the government on account of financial constraints and different priorities. The private sector if encouraged can put up necessary investment and corresponding managerial skills for the establishment and successful running of private elite institutions by making provisions for legitimate profit and freedom of academic/ administrative/financial autonomy.

Also what is worth noting is that Self Financing is not confined to private sector alone. State universities can also adopt such financing for development and excellence.

There are universities which are purely private with no government subsidy whatsoever. The universities of Yale, Princeton, Harvard, MIT,

Chicago, and Perdue amongst others are world famous and known for high quality education available to those who can afford to pay. Thus, there is a dual system of public and private education with traditional distinctions based primarily on the means of their financing and the nature of control. The United States is committed to preserving this dual system of higher education by maintaining both public as well as private institutions.

The higher education system in the U.K. shares some features with those in the USA. Self-governing nature of the universities and their administrative and financial autonomy are most important. The Universities of Oxford and Cambridge which are nearly 800 years old and the Universities of London and Durham founded in the early part of the 19th century, though not strictly private in the American context, are independent and self-governing academic bodies. Their funds, except those required for capital projects come from their own resources such as income from endowments, consultancy income of the faculty, donations, support from industry, voluntary subscriptions from alumni and most importantly tuition fees. It is high time that India should also think on these lines especially if the money earned can be "ploughed back" into the educational sector for its own improvement.

Reputed foreign universities should be invited and encouraged to establish campus/ campuses in India and run their activities, either alone or in collaboration with an Indian and/or foreign corporation/ university. The degrees could be awarded by the parent university. It is evident that the needed increase in our capacity for world class higher education cannot take place without a change of mindset of all the stakeholders, enabling legislation, supportive controlling bodies and good procedures.

There is no doubt about the fact that if there are a number of academic institutions nearby specializing in varied fields there will be academic advantage because of interaction. Also there will be healthy competition which will help in academic growth and development. Thus, private education and Education city are related. Till now education was dominated by State and Centre and no innovation like an education city was ever thought of. People here hardly have any motivation to do something different. Only a private initiative is feasible.

The demand for quality education is increasing and the number of aspirants is very high. Therefore there is a need to establish an Education city which will be an umbrella under which a student will find everything according to his need.[2]

Science & Technology and University

It is an accepted fact that all good and basic research which forms the basis of research and development has grown from universities. All Nobel laureates are almost exclusively from universities. All universities to a great extent contribute to science and technology. Developments in S&T are fundamentally altering the way people live, connect, correspond and communicate with profound effects on economic development. To promote technological advancements, developing countries should invest in quality education for youth, and continuous skills training for workers and managers.

Innovation is a break through that leads to social progress-it is a new, often unexpected and sometimes bold response to a need. Whether it comes in the form of a product, technology, service or policy, innovations transform social mores. The innovation process usually results from the cooperation of various actors who pool their knowledge, expertise and resources. Universities are places where critical thinking, invention, imagination and daring flourish. By continuing to push the boundaries of knowledge, challenging accepted notions, exploring original fields of research and combining approaches from various disciplines, universities are an inexhaustible source of the expertise and creativity that are central to the innovation process.

The growth of our economy, the health of our people and the security of our country depend on our scientific and technological competence. This is well understood and is reflected in the substantial support that the governments give to scientific research. This support is often devoted to immediate needs as perceived from time to time. Thus, the direction of scientific effort is shaped by society. Big discoveries have influenced society through new technological options, which have offered benefits to the mankind but have sometimes been used for harmful purposes as well. *Bertrand Russell* once said- "I am compelled to fear that science will be used to promote the power of dominant groups rather than to make men happy."

It is always very important to generate scientific pogrammes with societal inputs, infrastructure and intensity to enthuse the young minds; thus area specific approach is a must while taking up any project or programme, which is related to the problems of common man. Then only they would be a party to such an endeavour and assume responsibility for its effective implementation. A participatory approach and prior dialogue is necessary before conceptualizing any idea; this not only makes us familiar with the problems of masses but also strengthens the bond, helping in visualizing the possible impact of the programme.

India, with its tradition of excellent science, great scientists, scientific institutions, and rich cultural history that respects learning and excellence, has the potential to become a scientific power. Many factors for its greatness already exist viz. India possesses an immense pool of talented young minds many of whom have been attracted abroad, where they have made enormous contributions to science and technology. These young minds have strong ties with the country of its origin and are an important national resource that could greatly assist in the development of India. Secondly, the Indian economy is flourishing, now reaching unprecedented levels of growth.

India has to become science and technology superpower before it aspires to become an economic superpower. China is on its way to becoming a world leader, both in technology and in basic sciences. Realizing this aspiration requires investment. Despite repeated promises, the percentage of India's GDP devoted to research and development has remained at a paltry 0.9 per cent for 15 years — minuscule in comparison with developed countries: The US figure is 2.7 per cent; South Korea spends 4.4 per cent. In the last 15 years, Chinese investment in technology, higher education and the basic sciences has doubled. China now spends 2.1 per cent, and this percentage is rapidly increasing. In India industry needs to invest in universities so that they are in a position to be effective partners in progress.[3]

The science and education policy of most countries is based on the premise that the economic growth and prosperity are linked to higher education and research in science, engineering and technology and employment. Such countries are investing significantly to enhance the number and quality of the PhD s, as a part of the program to encourage higher education. Such an expansion has resulted in significant enhancement of the research output.

However, little can be achieved without investment. In the US, companies spend much on research and development of their products, but have realized that they cannot make truly new products without long-term investments in basic science that are best supported by the government. The recently created wealth in technological sectors of the Indian economy should in part be ploughed back to the country to support excellence in the basic sciences. The lack of necessary funds for investment in science guarantees failure; but money alone will not produce the desired results. If the R&D budget (relative to the GDP) and the GDP doubles, over the next decade, the resulting expansion of funds will only achieve its goals if there is fundamental reform in the structure of India's higher education and research institutions.

The predicament is that Indian science is burdened with an inflexible, irrational and outdated bureaucracy. There are lot of irrational bureaucratic regulations, such as severe restrictions on travel for young Indian scientists and for foreign collaborators, as well as forced retirement at a relatively early age for excellent, and sorely needed, scientific leaders. The fact is that the government is often unable to make right judgment of Quality.

The government and the bureaucracy alone cannot modify or rectify the existing state of affairs. The scientific and educational community must step in. Scientists and educators must demand and lobby for changes and they must also help in implementing these changes. Leading Indian scientists should engage in public discourse, participate in the necessary review and planning processes, create new institutions of excellence in research and education, and help raise the level of existing centers, thus said a Noble Prize Winner in Physics in the Indian Express. India does not lack brilliant young people who can create the science of the future, but they need to be given appropriate opportunities, visibility and engaged in decision-making. India has three national academies of science, but they play little role in either advising the government or representing the scientific community. The US benefits immensely from the advice it receives from the National Research Council, which produces over 400 reports a year for various fields/ activities. The Indian government also needs increased scientific input to address many urgent problems.

S & T are key drivers to development because technological and scientific revolution underpins economic advances, improvement in health systems, education and infrastructure. A Science park is an organization managed by specialized professionals, whose main aim is to increase the wealth of its community by providing the culture of innovation and the competitiveness of its businesses and knowledge based institutions. To enable these goals to be met a science park stimulates and manages the flow of knowledge and technology amongst universities, R & D institutions, companies and markets. It facilitates the creation and growth of innovation based companies through incubation and spin-off processes and provides other value added services together with high quality space and facilities.

Reforming governmental institutions is not simple, and allocating scarce resources for long-term payoffs is difficult. But both are necessary if India is to develop the science and technology necessary for its economic development and to take its rightful place among the scientific leaders of the world. Thus, if we focus our efforts around a clear enunciation of our goals arising from an understanding of our needs, endowments and competencies and all of the actors' viz. government, academia, scientific community, business, civil society and citizens- work together to realize a merit based accessible quality education system and excellence in research as a mission, India can definitely become an innovation super power by 2030.

The Vision of an Education City

A pioneering initiative for quality education can be taken by the central government or the state governments jointly with the corporate sector by establishing Special Educational Zones (SEZs) on the lines of Special Economic Zones in the country.

Special economic zones (also referred to as free zones) represent designated geographical areas within an economy, where business activity is subject to different rules from those prevailing in the rest of the economy. Those rules can pertain to investment conditions, trade, customs and taxes, etc. [Farole].[4] These zones can be established with different policy goals. The most common objective around the world is to attract foreign direct investment (FDI), as a means of boosting exports, links to global value chains (GVCs) and/or structural transformation of the economy. In countries suffering from high levels of unemployment, zones have been used to boost job creation by attracting investment in highly labour-intensive industries (for example in the Dominican Republic and Tunisia). Last but not least, zones have also been created to support wider economic reforms such as export diversification and upgrading (for example in the People's Republic of China, Korea and Chinese Taipei) as well as to serve as laboratories for experimentation with new policies and approaches that could, if the outcomes are satisfactory, be scaled up to the entire economy (for example in the People's Republic of China) (FIAS, 2008).[5]

The zones will be primarily dedicated to the development of higher professional educational institutions, R and D centers, state of the art laboratory/workshop/training facilities/convention centers etc. with all supportive infrastructures. These will attract investment in new establishments and new campuses of existing institutions. The biggest advantage of an Education city will be that a new education culture will emerge.

The suggested scheme for setting up of Special Educational Zones in the country will not only facilitate in the development of quality education and professional learning for the students of the country, it will also help export higher education, as the SEZs will attract foreign students who will pay in foreign currency to receive the domestically generated service of education in India. These earnings may in turn be ploughed back into educational investment for further improvement in quality and expansion of facilities. The proposed SEZs will provide internationally competitive environment in the cluster of education service providers with hassle free procedures of admission, teaching and interaction, practical classes and examination. Efficiency and transparency will be the hallmark of academic administration in the proposed SEZs.

The most distinctive features of the SEZs will be that these zones be treated as foreign territory for free operation of universities, colleges and institutes without government intervention in the regulation of fees and other authoritarian conditions. Instead government may assist them in establishment and see that they get free and competitive environment to work and start getting profit from producing the service of quality higher education. These zones should also be treated as duty free zones for producing and trading educational commodities and services.

An education city may be started by provision of land and basic facilities including access and communication, near a cluster of industry and business establishments. This can be financed under public private partnership. The city will have higher education institutions, R& D establishments, industrial parks (for nascent outfits) and central facilities, sports and recreational activity, centre for life skill development etc. and people/services/shops and establishments which support the working population (including students). The law and order and municipal services inclusive of gas/electricity etc. can be provided by a committee with representatives of the resident institutions, with a government official as chairman.

Education City is a vision of an entire city as a potential campus for learning and thus reframing education as something that happens everywhere in the city, not just in the four walled police-guarded educational institutions known as schools and colleges. The idea of an Education City is of an education system as an essential instrument for a citywide development and the city as a central instrument in the education system's development.

In an Education City there will be an open interface between industries and Universities. The industries will be free to exchange ideas with Universities, they will be able to communicate and convey their requirements and expectations to Universities to produce employable youths. There will be total empowerment of students, teachers, of the city, country and the world because now it will be a global village in true sense. Indians and foreigners would be absolutely free to move wherever they want to seek education and training. There will be no distinction between foreign and Indian degree. Every degree would be considered equivalent and of the same status. There would be free flow of information and expertise.

Surely it will be for the larger benefit of employers in India. Those who will pass will be able to take qualifying exam like NET, GATE which will lead to standardization. There will be no control on fees however, 10% of seats should not have fees more than in typical Indian Universities. Then there will be total autonomy. So far as Government jobs are concerned these degrees will be at par with other foreign degrees. Accreditation will depend on whether the universities want to get it from Indian or a foreign agency or a committee formed with both Indian and foreign members. Also if they do not want it, they would be free for that also. The syllabus, methodology, evaluation will be ultimately determined by them. The value of these degrees will be determined by the market. These universities may form their own Accreditation system. It will be totally an autonomous decision.

There will be common facilities like advanced labs, computing facilities and sports facilities that can be shared by everybody. Also there will be flow of faculty to different campuses. For students there will be transferable credits and the fees would be decided on credit basis. There will be emphasis on learning and overall empowerment of students. As far as possible six to eight weeks every year will be spent by a student in a corporate industry or business. Industry people will also be teaching in these Universities. Moreover this city should be approachable from an industrial city. University people should spend at least one semester every three to four years in industry. Industry can recruit people before a given course and employ them on completion of the course of their specifications. They can groom them according to their expectations. They can also give stipend during the course.

Academia-Industry-Business Interaction

Academia-industry interaction, a long felt need and often discussed subject has become all the more relevant and visible in the past few years, primarily because the complementary nature and mutual benefits of such an interaction have come to be appreciated by both sides. Universities and industry, which for long have been operating in separate domains, are converging to create synergies. This is primarily due to the need for innovation, creativity and continuous up-gradation of skills, required by the industry for keeping pace with technological development and competition. The constantly changing management paradigms in response to growing complexity of the business environment today, necessitate these two to come closer. Higher educational institutions not only contribute skilled human resource to business and industry, but also contribute in various intangible ways. The intersecting needs and mutually interdependent relationship requires identifying means of strengthening academia-industry partnership.[6]

Universities are situated on the crossroads of research, education and innovation. Indeed, according to a Communication from the Commission on "The Role of the Universities in the Europe of Knowledge" (COM (2003) 58) universities attract an increasing number of students; they employ 34% of the total number of researchers, and are responsible for 80% of the fundamental research pursued in Europe. However, compared to the U.S. knowledge is regarded as being not transferred and disseminated efficiently enough in Europe. In Commission's view cooperation between universities and the industry needs to be intensified and university-inventions geared more into innovations.

One of the problems which the Commission has identified is that in Europe fundamental research is often separate from its potential business applications resulting in companies' willingness to invest in applied rather than fundamental research. In general, the share of so-called contract based research is increasing, and universities are moving from exploratory science towards commercially profitable R&D, changing the scope of academic research. Meanwhile, the fundamental research takes potential business applications into consideration in the U.S. Nevertheless, universities work with the industry without compromising their guiding principles of teaching, research, open dissemination of information and serving the public. Also companies realize the benefits of being tapped into the university research pool through industry consortia membership, for instance, and sourcing new inventions as well as skilled workforce from them particularly in new areas such as biotechnology and biomedicine.

It is vital that knowledge flows from universities into business and society. Most technology transfer takes place through traditional ways viz. teaching, publications, and students, but there are two principal modes through which expertise possessed and developed by universities can flow directly to industry viz. licensing of intellectual property, and spin-off and start-up companies. The Education City can fulfil all the requirements for university-industry collaboration. Thus, it becomes important to discuss academic-industry-business interaction because an Education city provides an ideal venue for such an interaction.

Academia-Industry interface could be defined as interactive and collaborative arrangement between academic institutions and business corporations for the achievement of mutually inclusive goals and objectives. Traditionally, business schools look for placements and internships for their students and the industry for fresh recruits who are well trained and equipped with the right ***KSA*** (knowledge, skills and attitude) and empowered to contribute to the organization's growth. Bisoux[7] has explored the relationship between the academia and the industry. He states that corporations are placing growing emphasis on finding the "right person". This forces the business schools to think more carefully about the right person for the industry, and therefore the role of industry in the entire business school model becomes important.

The future of our country is going to be shaped in our classrooms since the survival of the domestic industry will depend on its technology leadership. India has emerged as one of the largest economies of the world and will continue its rapid urbanization and economic development with the aspiration of achieving double-digit growth in the coming years. Sustenance of this momentum largely depends upon our ability to leverage the vast pool of untapped human resource in our academic institutions for enhancing competitiveness in the global market place.

Today, there exists a huge gap between the rapidly evolving knowledge- skill needs of Indian business/industry and those provided by our higher educational system. There is a growing realization amongst the government, academic institutions and the industry, of the urgent need to bridge this gap. There is a need to adopt a holistic approach to the new age academia-industry interaction, which should address issues like improvement in governance of academic institutions and industry linkages, building centres of excellence, effective industry involvement in education related policy issues etc. Similarly, the academic fraternity needs to come out with their creative thoughts and share these with industry for their actualization.

More about academia-industry relation has been further elucidated in a specific reflection.

Educational Hubs in India

Making Indian higher education reach international standards is a top priority for Indian policy makers and education providers. A number of initiatives have been taken by policy makers and education agencies to promote the internationalization with the aim of putting Indian higher education on the global map; but unfortunately, only a handful of institutes represent the country in the global arena. One of the best ways to make education more focused and specialized would be to promote educational hubs all over India. These hubs do exist in India today but are largely heterogeneous in nature. Cities like Pune, Mumbai and Bangalore offer all possible avenues of education like medicine, engineering, hospitality and management across multi-disciplinary areas. However, the need of the hour is to have education hubs that are industry friendly.

Creating clusters of industries and academic institutions at the same location would go a long way in helping academia collaborate with their chosen industries. For example we could have engineering colleges and technical training schools around Chennai and Pune where there is a large presence of the automobile industry - both 2-wheeler and 4-wheeler. By the same logic, the IT cluster could be in Bangalore and Hyderabad while the hospitality cluster could be in Mumbai and Delhi. The advantages of getting more industry-based educational hubs would be that the students can get ample opportunities for on-the-job training during their period of study besides their regular internships. Secondly, faculty members too could be encouraged to take up live research projects and offer consultancy services in their areas of expertise. Thirdly, industry executives could use their spare time to take sessions for students via guest lectures and seminars and lastly, a lot of collaborative activities that could benefit the community at large could be done by industry and academic institutions.

The net outcome of the above would be that industry would be collaborating with academia to produce just the right kind of employees it needs. This would lead to increased productivity and result in more specialized research and new forays. Further, this leads to healthy competition among several institutions who are offering specialized courses of various types in a single domain. Thus, in the automobile cluster, though mechanical engineering is the main domain of study, related areas such as automobile engineering, production engineering, supply chain management, logistics and such could be valuable add-ons.

However, though we have several educational hubs today in many cities and clusters such as Pune, Mangalore, Bangalore, and Warangal, these are not homogenous in nature and have multiple programmes across every possible stream. Thus, these are centers of education but are not industry specific. While we cannot change the existing set-up overnight, we need to consciously plan in a way so that future educational hubs are based on the above model. Of course there is a difference between an Educational hub and Education city. In an Education city there is more interaction and competition.

Locations such as Raipur, Indore, Nasik, Nagpur, Bhubaneswar and Baroda have ample scope to set up educational hubs of excellence that could be specialization driven. Besides, we need to ensure that world-class quality standards such as those of ACBSP or QS are maintained at the highest levels. However, one must remember that if we need to attract students from all over the world, we must ensure that the sanitation and infrastructure should be world class. These cities should be further developed to be student friendly and an attractive choice for them like well-established B type cities are Pune, Ahmedabad, Coimbatore and Pondicherry to name a few. Thus, before we go global, we need to put the local infrastructure in place.[8] It is obvious that the hubs are a far cry from an education city.

Our experience with creating these hubs has been mixed. The Madhya Pradesh government took the initiative for rapid privatization of higher education in the state in 2010. For this purpose, Chief Minister Shivraj Singh Chauhan decided to set up Special Education Zones (SEdZ) in the State on the lines of Special Economic Zones (SEZ) in consultation with the State Higher Education Minister and chief Secretary of the State. The SEdZ will promote the setting up of private universities and educational institutions. It was decided that national level educational institutions will be established at these places. For this purpose land was selected to be acquired in Manikharaia, Bahauri and village in Bhopal district. Surveys about availability of land in Sagar, Raisen and Vidisha districts were made. Even letter of intent was issued for setting up private universities at Raghogarh, Gwalior and Bhopal. Since 2000, Government of Madhya Pradesh was making attempt to set up Special Education Zones (**SEdZs**) but no investor has shown interest. In 2008, Government allocated 110 acre land to Mr. Anil Ambani's "Dhiru Bhai Ambani Memorial Trust (DAMT)" in Bhopal district but the trust abandoned the project, while the first SEdZ was decided to be established in Bhopal and another one was proposed to be set up near Ujjain.[9]

Honorable Chief Minister of Haryana Bhupinder Singh Hooda opened doors to a new era of education hubs in Haryana when he inaugurated Rajiv Gandhi Education City at Sonepat in 2013. The campus houses some of the country's best educational institutions and Universities set up over a vast expanse of 2000 acres. Shri Hooda said, "Education and industrial growth are indispensable for speedy development of the state and the Haryana Government has been consistently making efforts in this regard. The State Government is also taking effective measures for the development of Rai, Kundli and Sonepat in order to meet the anticipated growth along the Kundli-Manesar-Palwal expressway, which will play a crucial role in overall development of the area." Along with these major steps undertaken by the State Government to promote higher education in Haryana, a provision was also made to set up an International University Centre in the Education City.[10]

Publicization at National and International Level

India is the second largest source of internationally mobile students around the world. According to the UNESCO data, in 2015, nearly

234,000 Indian students were enrolled in universities and colleges abroad. In contrast, Indian universities and colleges were host to nearly 39,000 degree-seeking international students. The Government of India is showing interest in enhancing the attractiveness of India as a destination for international students. At the same time, some Indian institutions are keen on making use of the 15% additional seats available to them for enrolling foreign students. It also helps in enhancing global reputation and global rankings of some institutions. There are also extreme examples. Some reputed university network is said to spend 25% of their revenue on advertisement.

However, India faces increasing competition as many other destinations have already been active in creating government policies and institutional capacities for attracting global talent. For example, in 2015, Malaysia and China hosted more than 60,000 and 123,000 degree-seeking international students, respectively.

The recent FICCI Higher Education Summit convened institutional leaders, policy makers, and education experts to deliberate on opportunities for and challenges in attracting foreign students to India. Shobha Mishra Ghosh, Senior Director at FICCI noted that the Indian higher education system is the largest in the world in terms of the number of institutions and second largest in terms of student enrollment. Building on this scale, the government is working towards introducing reforms to promote India as a global education hub. She mentioned several initiatives, including the National Institutional Ranking Framework (NIRF) to set global benchmarks for the quality of education, as well as the introduction of friendlier visa policies and processes for students, ongoing work towards mutual recognition of degrees, and support for institutional partnerships and exchange programs.

At the same time, there are challenges to overcome in working towards ambitious goals in a competitive and a complex environment for attracting international students. Francisco Marmolejo, Lead, Global Solutions Group on Tertiary Education and Lead Education Specialist for India for The World Bank Group said that for foreign institutions, connecting with Indian institutions is not easy. This is not only because of the large number of institutions but also due to significant diversity and variation in the quality of institutions. He encouraged Indian institutions to go beyond connections in Europe, Australia, and North America, mostly in English-speaking countries, to emerging nations in South America and Africa.

Marmolejo also said that India must work towards building "more national and institutional capacity to outreach potential students abroad." This includes "assuring a more consistent and coordinated presence of India in international education student fairs, organizations and events; a detailed review and improvement of migratory and administrative procedures related to mobility of students; and fostering flexibility at the institutional level to recognize learning acquired abroad, among other actions."

Some strategies need to be worked upon for publicity at International level. For this firstly there is a need to enhance the country image. International education is often an expensive, one-time investment for students and their families. This makes the country image a critical factor in considering a destination. India does not rank high as a destination in regards to safety, hygiene, and quality of life. Some of these factors are very critical from a student's perspective. Institutions must help prospective international students understand the value of being part of India's story and articulate the broader opportunities it offers as a destination. Secondly, given the cost and distances, international students try to find indicators that can minimize their risks of studying abroad. Despite extensive information available on the Internet, there is a lack of trusted information that aims to help students make informed choices. Students also struggle in making sense of jargons and comparing information across institutions. There is a need to provide trusted, unbiased and updated information to students.

Thirdly, international students differ in characteristics and motivations to go abroad. These motivations are affected by many factors, including financial resources and academic preparedness. For example, a student aiming for Harvard is very different from someone considering some top-ranked institution in India. A deeper understanding of the various international student segments and their decision-making processes will result in more effective strategies and outcomes. Lastly, most of the Indian institutions lack global recognition and rankings. Thus, they spend their resources in over-promising through glitzy websites and advertisements without building core capabilities. They often overlook the role of faculty and staff in delivering a superior experience and do not invest proportionally in support services. Institutions must invest in shaping international students' experiences as good experiences create successful brand ambassadors who in turn spread word of mouth.

Thus, some Indian institutions have the right blend of ambition and potential to attract international students. However, realizing the goals will require proactive and informed strategies which are designed to support student success.[11]

Impact of Globalization

Education, Science and Technology are basically global in nature and therefore we should have a variety of educational systems. Interaction with each other is possible only if our education and teachers are drawn from different sources. India has the potential of becoming a global hub for providing high-end manufacturing services to the world. There is still a need to have a clear and unambiguous perception in the direction of leveraging strength towards actualization of excellence. There is a need to create synergies between efficiency, objectives and energy of Indian industries with creativity, knowledge and competence of Indian academia to exploit emerging opportunities. A corollary to this thought is that India should strive to become a global hub for excellent education and research, in conformance with the needs of the industry. **And this aim can be achieved by establishing an Education City.**

Some of the benefits accruing to the industry with this interaction would be using the academic knowledge base to improve industrial cost, quality and competitive dimensions, reducing dependence on foreign know-how, expenditure on internal R&D and updating and upgrading the knowledge base of the industry's professionals through professional development programmes designed by the academia cum industry. The faculty's exposure to industry leads to improved curricula and widened and deepened teaching perspectives resulting in professional graduates of a high calibre to man the industry. The academia would also be benefited with the satisfaction of seeing their knowledge and expertise being used for socially useful and productive purposes, widening and deepening of the curricula and developing the perspectives of teachers and researchers and earning additional resources for a system severely constrained in this regard. Securing training and final placements for students are much easier on account of the recognition earned from and the relationships established with industry.

The accreditation process for technical institutions (offering engineering, management and computer courses) should specifically highlight the potential and capabilities for training, problem-oriented research and consultancy and give a separate star rating in this aspect in addition to the overall institutional rating now being given. This should also be given for social sciences disciplines such as economics, commerce, psychology and sociology.

Though focusing on international collaboration as a priority in India by the higher education sector has gained momentum recently, individual institutional initiatives in this direction are not new; there are quite a few instances of fruitful international cooperation between Indian and foreign Universities in academics and research. With the increased attention it has been getting in recent years, an increasing number of Indian universities are now actively seeking opportunities to network with institutions and research teams worldwide. But to sustain competitiveness in the globalized environment the academic culture and processes of the organization should exhibit a distinctive character of 'in built flexibility' in the approach and policies particularly in its offerings and programme structures. Without such flexibility the university system will find it increasingly difficult to adjust to the various external factors originating outside their national boundaries.

Higher education systems, policies and institutions are being transformed by globalization, it can be described as "the widening, deepening and speeding up of worldwide interconnectedness" (Held et al.)[12] In global knowledge economies, higher education institutions are more important than ever as a medium for a wide range of cross border relationships and continuous global flow of people, information, knowledge, technologies products and financial capital. "All universities are not (particularly) international, but all are subject to the same processes of globalization-partly as subjects, or key agents of globalization" Scott.[13] A generation ago, international relations were largely marginal to the day to day operations of institutions and systems, except in scientific research. Now the growing impact of global environment is inescapable. In many nations, international mobility, global comparison, bench-marking and ranking and the internationalization of institutions and system are key policy themes; the governments and university leaders are preoccupied by strategies of cross border cooperation and competition.

Globalization of higher education has enabled the students, teachers and researchers to move freely and choose the organizations, networks and communities of their liking across the countries. Examples of globalization of higher education are the creation of international student exchange programs, the adaptation to a unified course-credit system, and the conformation to international quality assessments. Such acts of globalization, bringing an international dimension to higher education, can be seen as first steps towards embracing diversity and achieving higher levels of complexity and speed. Another impact of globalization is the emergence of a global education market-place where each institution has to compete for funds, faculty and students. This growing competition increasingly takes place on a worldwide scale, as is indicated by joint degree offerings among institutions in two or more countries, off-shoring through franchising or branch openings, using the Internet as a new delivery channel.

Conclusion

To conclude, an all-round excellence of higher education institutes and supporting linkages is essential for the health and progress of science and its utilization. It is only when faculty, students, research and curricula are all aligned with industry/business that a healthy interaction and the synergy between academia and industry can take place. To realize the Vision of India as an Innovation Hot Spot, first we need to realize long term academia-industry collaborative relationships with open access to and resources free of intellectual property (IP) entanglements and secondly, to put in place better integration of the corporate world with higher educational and research institutions to create a pipeline for skills that will support growth industries. Thirdly, we need to encourage multidisciplinary collaboration among business, government, academia and R&D laboratories, thereby creating an environment that supports technological development, which is associated with and driven by industry needs.

Fourthly, we should recognize the contribution of young researchers to the vitality and quality of the research system and put in place more programmes for support of young researchers. Fifthly, we can enhance significantly publicly funded research that reaches out to the market by engaging corporate executives as champions. Further we should take up in collaboration with concerned government Ministries the modernization and up gradation of technology in use by the small and medium enterprises. Also we need to encourage the formation of international R&D, technology and innovation consortia between Indian and foreign entities and lastly, provide tax incentives to businesses which collaborate with academia and R&D researchers.

Last but not the least there is an urgent need to take up a pioneering initiative for quality education by the central government or the government jointly with the corporate sector by establishing Special Educational Zones (SEZs) on the lines of Special Economic Zones in the country. The zones will be primarily dedicated to the development of higher professional educational institutions, R and D centers, state of the art laboratory/workshop/training facilities/convention centers etc. with all supportive infrastructures. These will attract investment in new establishments and new campuses of existing institutions. The biggest advantage of an Education city will be that a new education culture will emerge.

Specific References

1. Sodha, M.S., and Reena Srivastava, (2004), Private Universities: Challenges and Opportunities, in K.B. Powar and K.L. Johar (Eds), *Private Initiatives in Higher Education*, Pp. 153-164, Sneh Prakashan, Yamunanagar.
2. Sodha, M.S. and M. Muzammil, (2008), *For Profit provision of Higher Education*, University News, 46 (01), Pp. 07-13.
3. https://qz.com/india/771498/if-india-wants-to-become-a-superpower-it-has-to-stop-trying-to-become-the-next-china/

4. Farole, T. (2011), "Special Economic Zones in Africa: Comparing Performance and Learning from Global Experience", World Bank, Washington, DC.
5. http://www.oecd.org/south-east-europe/SEZ_WB_2017.pdf
6. *Soni, R., (2007). Intellectuals' Expectations from a University: An Exploratory Study. Ph.D. Thesis, Department of Education, University of Lucknow, Lucknow.*
7. Bisoux Tricia, *"New Directions in Global Education*", Bized January/ February 2003 AACSB Publication, pp. 34-37.
8. Prof R S S Mani, Vice President -Institutional Development, ITM Group of Institutions https://www.indiatoday.in/education-today/featurephilia/story/special-education-zones-for-academia-industry-collaboration-1097382-2017-11-30.
9. http://www.thehindu.com/news/national/other-states/M.P.-to-set-up-Special-Education Zones/article16189390.ece
10. https://www.business-standard.com/article/press-releases/manav-rachna-university-launched-at-rajiv-gandhi-education-city-112061000037_1.html
11. https://blogs.economictimes.indiatimes.com/HigherEdChange/building-a-capacity-to-attract-international-students-to-indian-universities-and-colleges/
12. Held, David; McGraw, Anthony; Gold blat, David; Perraton, Jonathan (1999). Global Transformations: Politics, Economics and Culture. Stanford, CA: Stanford UniversityPress, Stanford.
13. Scott, Peter (1998). "Massification, Internationalization and Globalization. In: Scott, P. (ed.). The Globalization of Higher Education. Buckingham: The Society for Research into Higher Education/ Open University Press. Pages 108-29.

General References

1. Ananth, M. S., (2011), 'University Research Parks', *Frontiers in Science and Technology: Abstracts of Plenary Sessions,* at the 98th Indian Science Congress, January 3-7.
2. Burke, Joseph C., and Henrik Minassians, (2003), *Performance Reporting: Real Accountability or Accountability "Lite."* Albany, New York: Nelson A. Rockefeller Institute of Government.
3. Planning Commission, Government of India, (2008), *Public-Private Partnership in Higher and Technical Education*, Draft Consultation Paper, GOI, New Delhi.
4. Powar, K.B., and Johar, K.L., (2004), Private Higher Education: An Overview, in K.B. Powar and K.L. Johar (Eds), *Private Initiatives in Higher Education*, Pp. 167-201, Sneh Prakashan, Yamunanagar.

5. Powar K.B., and Bhalla, Veena, (2004), Private Initiatives in Professional Higher Education, in K.B. Powar and K.L. Johar (Eds), *Private Initiatives in Higher Education*, Pp. 11-28, Sneh Prakashan, Yamunanagar.
6. Salmi, Jamil, (2008), *The Challenge of Establishing World-Class Universities*. Washington DC: The World Bank.
7. Sanyal, B.C. and Johnstone, B., (2011), International Trends in Public and Private Financing of Higher Education, *Prospects*, 41: 157-175.
8. Teixeira, P., Jongbloed, B., and D. Dill, (2004), *Markets in Higher Education: Rhetoric or Reality*. New York: Springer Publications.
9. Wertz, Richard D. (2000), *Issues and Concerns in the Privatization and Outsourcing of Campus Services in Higher Education*. New York, New York: National Center for the Study of Privatization in Higher Education.
10. Wikipedia, (2008), Public-private partnership, http:/en.wikipedia.org/wiki/public-private partnership.
11. Article by Noble Prize Winner in Physics in Indian Express. http://indianexpress.com/article/opinion/columns/discover-invent-in-india/#sthash.Cdr7M1HY.dpuf

Reflection - 3

Entrepreneurship in Higher Education

Introduction

An organization comes into existence only because of the efforts put in by an individual, who would be prepared to assume responsibility of leading the enterprise. For that, the individual must have a special quality that is known as entrepreneurship. Entrepreneurship as an economic activity emerges and functions in the sociological and cultural environment. It could be conceived as an individual's free choice activity or a social group's occupation or profession.

The basic concept of entrepreneurship entails an effective and deliberate inner urge to take risk in terms of uncertainties and an intuition. In short, an entrepreneur shows wisdom to jump into untested waters and face the consequences, with a strong self-conviction that he will successfully encounter the sharks and befriend the dolphins. The common definition for an entrepreneur is a person, who organizes, manages, and takes the risk of running a business or enterprise. The entrepreneurs perform a vital function in economic development of a nation. They have been referred to as the human agents needed to mobilize capital, to exploit natural resources, often develop innovative products or concepts, to create markets and to carry on business. It may be construed that the entrepreneurial contribution spells the difference between prosperity and poverty among nations.

The importance of entrepreneurs to progress cannot be more crisply expressed than the statement – no entrepreneur, no development. The inactivity or scarcity of entrepreneurs has for sometimes been the factor seen by many Asian countries as a major hindrance to economic development. The availability of abundant natural resources, skilled and unskilled labour, and capital has not proven itself sufficient enough to result in a surge of entrepreneurial zeal among the people. One of the important inputs in any economic development of a country is entrepreneurship. More the entrepreneurship activities, better the development. Entrepreneurship is the life blood of any economy and it applies very much to a developing economy like India.

The idea of infusing entrepreneurship in education has spurred much enthusiasm in the last few decades. A myriad of effects has been stated to result from this, such as economic growth, job creation and increased societal resilience, as well as individual growth, better school engagement and improved equality. Putting this idea into practice has however posed significant challenges alongside the stated positive effects. Lack of time and resources, teachers' fear of commercialism, impeding educational structures, assessment difficulties and lack of definitional clarity are some of the challenges encountered by practitioners, trying to infuse entrepreneurship in the education sector. Entrepreneurship is not just about economic growth or jobs, or knowledge production and science in universities. "Those are very important, but entrepreneurship is about a much wider range of activities. It is primarily a social activity. "It is about social justice. How can we re-establish at mass level a spirit of entrepreneurship – the ability of people and communities to produce high levels of self-sustainability?" Before we discuss about the role of higher education in entrepreneurship, we will understand a little in detail about its concept and meaning.

What is Entrepreneurship?

The definition of entrepreneurship has been debated among scholars, educators, researchers and policy makers since the concept was first given in the early 1700's. The term "entrepreneurship" comes from the French verb *"entreprendre"* and the German word *"unternehmen"*, both mean to "undertake". By grave and Hofer[1] defined the entrepreneurial process as 'involving all the functions, activities, and actions associated with perceiving of opportunities and creation of organizations to pursue them'. Joseph Schumpeter introduced the modern definition of 'entrepreneurship' in 1934. According to Schumpeter[2], "the carrying out of new combinations we call 'enterprise'," and "the individuals whose function it is to carry them out we call 'entrepreneurs'." Schumpeter tied entrepreneurship to the creation of five basic "new combinations" namely: introduction of a new product, introduction of a new method of production, opening of a new market, the conquest of a new source of supply and carrying out of a new organization of industry.

Peter Drucker[3] proposed that 'entrepreneurship' is a practice. What this means is that entrepreneurship is not a state of being nor is it characterized by making plans that are not acted upon. Entrepreneurship begins with action viz. creation of new organization. This organization may or may not become self-sustaining and in fact, may never earn significant revenues. But, when individuals create a new organization, they have entered the entrepreneurship paradigm. Entrepreneur is a borrowed word from the French language that refers to a person who undertakes and operates a new venture, and assumes some accountability for the inherent risks. Being in business or being an entrepreneur is about taking risks and confronting challenges. Entrepreneurs build companies that are specifically crafted to exploit a particular opportunity. This gives them an advantage over older companies that were designed in response to challenges of the past and must change to adapt to today's requirements. Entrepreneurs can build new companies. They can also rejuvenate existing companies via buyouts and turnarounds. They can also build new companies inside existing companies, which can be called corporate entrepreneurship.

Entrepreneurship is a complex term that's often defined simply as running your own business. But there's a difference between a "business owner" and an "entrepreneur," and although one can be both, **what distinguishes entrepreneurship is a person's attitude**." Entrepreneurship is much broader than the creation of a new business venture," said Bruce Bachenheimer, a clinical professor of management and executive director of the Entrepreneurship Lab at Pace University. "At its core, it is a mind-set, a way of thinking and acting. It is about imagining new ways to solve problems and create value."

"An entrepreneur is someone who can take any idea, whether it be a product and/or service, and have the skillset, will and courage to take extreme risk to do whatever it takes to turn that concept into reality and not only bring it to market but make it a viable product and/or service that people want or need," said MJ Gottlieb, co-founder of consulting firm Hustle Branding and author of "How to Ruin a Business Without Really Trying", Morgan James Publishing, 2014[4].

Wide and narrow views on entrepreneurship

Being entrepreneurial can mean many things to many people. A common concept according to Gartner[5] is that entrepreneurship is about entrepreneurial individuals creating innovative organizations that grow and create value, either for the purpose of profit or not. But entrepreneurship does not have to include the creation of new organizations, it can also occur in existing organizations (Shane and Venkataraman).[6] It is not only limited to the entrepreneurial individual, but also to entrepreneurial opportunities and the relation between the individual and the opportunity, i.e. the individual-opportunity nexus as described by Shane.[7] Stevenson and Jarillo[8] define entrepreneurship as "a process by which individuals - either on their own or inside organizations - pursue opportunities without regard to the resources they currently control. Bruyat and Julien[9] use a constructivist approach and propose a definition incorporating not only the entrepreneur, but also the new value created, the environment within which it takes place, the entrepreneurial process itself and the links between these constructs over time. They also propose the terms "individual" and "entrepreneur" to represent teams when applicable. Entrepreneurial spirit is characterized by innovation and risk-taking, and is an essential part of a nation's ability to succeed in an ever changing and increasingly competitive global marketplace. An individual attempts to realize his vision, irrespective of available resources. In other words an entrepreneur does more with less resource.

Characteristics of a Successful Entrepreneur

Some business experts suggest that the entrepreneurial drive is innate, a trait acquired at birth, while others believe that anyone can become an entrepreneur. Whether a person is born to it or develops it, there are characteristics and traits required for successful entrepreneurship including:

- **Passion** - Talk to successful entrepreneurs and you'll nearly always hear the word passion when they describe what they do. Following your passion is one of the best predictors of success.
- **Independent thinking** - Entrepreneur often thinks outside the box and is not discouraged by others who might question his/her ideas.
- **Optimism** - It's difficult to succeed at anything if we don't believe in a good outcome. Entrepreneurs are dreamers and believe their ideas are possible, even when they seem unattainable.
- **Self-confidence** - This is not to say entrepreneurs never have self-doubt, but they're able to overcome it, and believe they can achieve their goal.
- **Resourceful and problem solvers** - Lack of assets, knowledge, and resources are common, but entrepreneurs are able to get what they need or figure out how to use what they've got in order to reach their goals. They never let problems and challenges get in the way, and instead find ways to achieve success despite hardships.
- **Tenacity and ability to overcome hardship** - Entrepreneurs don't quit at the first, second or even hundredth obstacle. For them, failure is not an option, so they continue to work toward success, even when things go wrong.
- **Vision**- Some of the more stringent definitions of entrepreneurship include vision as a necessary element. It helps to know your end goal when you start. Further, vision is the fuel that propels you forward toward your goal.
- **Focus** - It's easy in this fast paced, constant info-in-your-face world to get distracted. This is especially true for business start-ups that often get side-tracked by the, shiny object syndrome (i.e. products and services that promise fast results), or bogged down in unimportant busy work. Successful entrepreneurs are focused on what will bring desired results.

- **Action oriented** - Entrepreneurs don't expect something from nothing and they don't wait for things to happen. They are doers. They overcome challenges and avoid procrastination.

Higher Education and Entrepreneurship

Stimulating innovative and growth-oriented entrepreneurship is a key economic and societal challenge to which universities and colleges have much to contribute. University is a public institution meant to serve the public cause. The 21st-century university will engage more fully with society than at any time in its past. Our value proposal is that knowledge enables a better tomorrow. We realize that promise through the translation of great discoveries into new cures, new technologies and new practices. We also recognize that promise by training young men and women, but at the same time instilling in them the notion that ideas have power in their application, and that knowledge enables progress through action. Entrepreneurship, the translation of ideas into products and actions, will be at the core of the University of Tomorrow (and even today).

Numerous studies on the relationship between Higher Education Institutions and industry have examined the economic value of university activity, the contribution of staff and students to the economy, university offshoots and the development of entrepreneurship education. As organizations in society, universities provide a structure for human interaction with the wider environment. This structure is afforded through the education of students for, primarily, the future workplace, pure and applied research, skills training and increasingly the outreach with industry and the wider community of people and organizations. In this attempt to generate higher levels of human interaction and act as agents of change, universities adopt particular governance structures, sets of skills and strategies; they use these to implement the rules or constraints that shape the different forms of human interaction meant to make a contribution to the economy.

Entrepreneurship is a key driver of our economy. Wealth and a high majority of jobs are created by small businesses started by entrepreneurially minded individuals, many of whom go on to create big businesses. People exposed to entrepreneurship frequently express that they have more opportunity to exercise creative freedom, higher self-esteem, and an overall greater sense of control over their own lives. Many experienced business people political leaders, economists, and educators believe that fostering a robust entrepreneurial culture will maximize individual and collective economic and social success on a local, national, and global scale. Entrepreneurship helps in the introduction and dissemination of new methods and technology. It also builds the community network.

Entrepreneurship Education at Universities

Liberalization and privatization of education, leading to freedom of thought and action and responsiveness to the emerging environment are seen as a precondition for entrepreneurship and economic development. Education plays a two-fold role in the development of entrepreneurship. One of these is to create the right attitudes in individuals and the other is to develop knowledge and skills relevant for entrepreneurship.

While educators of primary and secondary levels have an opportunity to foster entrepreneurial attitudes that could lead to individuals taking up an entrepreneurial career later, the quality of entrepreneurship could be substantially improved by the technical, entrepreneurial and managerial knowledge and skills imparted at the higher education level. Such knowledge and skills can help the new endeavour survive and grow against all odds, particularly those created by its "liability of newness as well as smallness."

Only in recent times has higher education begun to be perceived as an instrument of entrepreneurship promotion; for a long time, the two kept a distance. Universities rarely considered entrepreneurship to be a discipline with a body of knowledge worthy of being taught and learned. This was to be expected as the word entrepreneurship is of fairly recent origin. It was only in 1803 that the French economist J.B. Say[10] coined the word entrepreneur to distinguish it from the term 'investor' on the one hand and 'manager' on the other. It was only in the middle of the 20th century that entrepreneurship research picked up momentum. The first academic programme in entrepreneurship was started by Harvard University in 1945 as several industrial enterprises were created to serve war needs. Since then many Higher Education institutions have recognized that entrepreneurship courses could indeed be an effective tool for them to stimulate the economy through their graduates, who would start up new ventures and thereby create wealth and provide employment.

In a comprehensive analysis of the learning orientations in university education as compared to the learning needs of entrepreneurs, Gibb has identified a series of mismatches. The basic difference is that universities focus on imparting knowledge and information as against entrepreneur's need for developing implementation skills. The long traditions of imparting knowledge oriented education through Higher Education institutions has come in the way of faculty developing any competence in imparting skill-oriented education. As a consequence it is natural for entrepreneurs not to trust such institution or the programme they offer.

Innovations in Entrepreneurship Education

University programmes for entrepreneurship can be classified into two categories:

1. Academic programmes, part or full in entrepreneurship offered to first year students aspiring to be entrepreneurs.
2. Training programmes offered to active entrepreneurs with a view to improving their effectiveness.

The experience of universities offering full time degree programmes in entrepreneurship has not been very encouraging. Graduation in entrepreneurship has not yet become an attractive proposition for youth, partly because a degree of this kind will not guarantee entrepreneurial success. Though such a guarantee is not available for typical management degrees either, the failure of a management graduate in an established organization is not as disastrous as the failure of an entrepreneur in his or her own venture. Certain societies are better able to accommodate failure than others and where there is no such accommodation; the social and economic cost of failure is higher than the cost of settling for the meagre rewards of an ordinary job. Universities in such risk-averse cultures are hardly likely to educate their students to consider failure an option, even in its most abstract form.

Apart from the Entrepreneurship Cells present in colleges, there are several educational institutions in India that offer various programme/ courses to support entrepreneurial learning. For convenience and awareness we are providing a partial list of these educational institutions.

- Amity Business School (Noida) – M.B.A in Entrepreneurship
- D Y Patil, Mumbai University (Mumbai) – M.B.A in Entrepreneurship Management
- Delhi Business School (Delhi) - specialization in Entrepreneurship & Business
- Deshpande Foundation (Hubli) – Master of Social Entrepreneurship
- EMPI's centre for Global Business Entrepreneurship & Research (Delhi) - specialization in Global Business & Entrepreneurship
- Entrepreneurship Development Institute of India (Gandhinagar) – specialization in Business Entrepreneurship
- Entrepreneurship Development Institute of India (Gandhinagar) – specialization in Development Sector and Social Entrepreneurship
- Entrerprise Development Institute (Kolkata) – Diploma in Entrepreneurship
- European Management Institute (Delhi) – MBA in Entrepreneurship Development
- IIM Bangalore (NSRCEL) – specialization in Entrepreneurs & Family Businesses
- IIM Bangalore (NSRCEL) – specialization in Women Entrepreneurs
- IIM Indore - specialization in Family owned Businesses & Entrepreneurship
- IIPM (Delhi) – B.B.A/M.B.A in Planning and Entrepreneurship
- Indraprastha College of Management & Technology (Jodhpur) – specialization in Entrepreneurship & Business Management
- Infinity Business School (Gurgoan) – specialization in Entrepreneurship
- Institute of Marketing and Management (Delhi) - specialization in Entrepreneurship
- International College of Fashion (Delhi) – M.B.A in Entrepreneurship (Fashion)

- ISB (Goldman Sachs - Hyderabad) – Certificate course in Women Entrepreneurs
- ISB(Wadhwani Foundation - Hyderabad) – specialization in Global Growth Entrepreneurship
- JGI Group (Bangalore) – specialization in Entrepreneurship, Entre &Mgt,
- KIIT School of Management (Bhubaneshwar) – M.B.A in Entrepreneurship
- Kohinoor Business School (Pune) – M.B.A in Entrepreneurship
- L.N. Welingkar (Mumbai) – specialization in Family Managed Business
- Lal Bahadur Sastri Institute of Management - specialization in Entrepreneurship
- Master School of Management (Meerut) – specialization in Entrepreneurship
- Mudra Institute of Communication (Ahmedabad) – specialization in Communications, Management & Entrepreneurship
- Nirma Institute of Management (Ahmedabad) – M.B.A in Family Business and Entrepreneurship
- NMIMS (Mumbai) – M.B.A in Social Entrepreneurship
- Rai Business School (Delhi) – specialization in Planning and Entrepreneurship
- SPJIMR (Mumbai) – specialization in Family Managed Business
- Tata Institute of Social Sciences (Mumbai) – M.A in Social Entrepreneurship
- Xavier Institute of Management & Entrepreneurship (Bangalore) – specialization in Entrepreneurship Development
- XLRI (Jamshedpur) - Certificate in Entrepreneurship Management

Entrepreneurship is an adaptable toolset for solving problems and scaling solutions and there is certainly no shortage of problems to solve in our increasingly complex world. From addressing the global water crisis to lessening industry's environmental impact, student inventors have ample opportunities to create solutions to 21st century problems. That's why there's a critical need to cultivate innovators and entrepreneurs that are well-equipped to solve the world's biggest challenges and create lasting impact. Yet much remains to be done. Not all inventor entrepreneurs have access to the appropriate training and support to even test their idea, let alone take it to market. Fortunately, student innovators often are able to get the appropriate scientific, technical, and entrepreneurial help from faculty or university ecosystem.

By taking action in specific ways, we can enable faculty and academic institutions to support student innovators in taking their first steps toward turning societal challenges into opportunities for economically accessible solutions through innovation and entrepreneurship.

For this, students should be provided with a greater understanding of the overall innovation process and the possible pathways to develop compelling innovations and bring them to scale. This is possible through a learning-by-doing approach. Educators can use experiential learning opportunities within and alongside the curriculum that expose students to the process of inventing solutions to problems that matter. As these emergent innovations are cultivated, engagement with the communities beyond the university can provide relevant advising, mentoring, and support.

One example of a successful model is the University of Colorado Colorado Springs (UCCS) undergraduate and graduate certificate programs in innovation. Through a Venture Well Faculty Grant, UCCS developed a new curriculum for a graduate degree program in innovation to provide students with hands-on training that allows them to investigate new ideas. The program also includes a new on-campus incubator and co-working space called the E-Zone that supports the strongest student teams as they focus on developing their innovations into new start-ups.

Successful student innovators and entrepreneurs do not operate in a vacuum. They need to have access to a range of resources viz. courses, trainings, mentorships, networks, funds on and off campus. Developing a product or company requires engagement with an ecosystem of business connections and resources. Rather than trying to re-create this artificially within the campus, emerging teams of innovators should connect to these resources directly. Facilitating those connections is part of creating a successful and engaged program. The same can be said for faculty trying to integrate innovation and entrepreneurship on campus.

Entrepreneurship in Higher Education: Some Case Studies

We will best illustrate three modes of entrepreneurship in education by examples. The first viz. NCU is an opportunity driven private initiative; the second is a large scale initiative. The third one is a hybrid model, where the initiative has been taken by a university on the basis of usually available facilities. This may be called **hybrid model**.

North Cap University, Gurgaon

In nineties Haryana was increasingly getting industrialized and it was hard to get admission to even an average engineering institution. At the same time the faculty at nearby IIT Delhi started getting retired in significant numbers. A group of young entrepreneurs recognized this as a unique opportunity for establishment and growth of an institution for quality education in engineering and management. Thus was born the Institute of Technology and Management at Gurgaon near Delhi which grew in size and structure by utilizing the retired faculty from IIT Delhi and also having faculty on lecture basis. With focus on quality and limited by generated resources the institution, now a University is moving ahead.

Amity University Network

The first university (with full scale operation) of the Amity network became functional in 2003 with campuses at NOIDA and Lucknow. Since then the network has grown to have nine university campuses in India and eight Campuses abroad. At Amity a student may get a degree from Amity and certificates from universities in UK and USA; the programme requires some attendance at the UK and US universities. Students also visit companies, industry and other universities abroad. The Amity network is probably the largest private educational initiative in the country.

A Case Study in Institution Building: Devi Ahilya Vishwa-vidalaya (1988-92)

The university started functioning in 1964, with the taking over of the affiliation of colleges in Indore district, which were previously affiliated to Vikram University Ujjain. By 1988, the university teaching departments had aggregate student strength of around 600, spread over ten schools of studies (Education, Economics, Management, Computer Science, Physics, Chemistry, Mathematics, Statistics, Life Science) Sponsored research projects of around Rs.10 lac, helped research in basic sciences. An understaffed University Science Instrumentation Centre existed on paper only; the initial grants of the centre were divided among different schools of study and almost no engineering/technical staff or services were available. The university had two campuses-one in the heart of city with an area of 10acres and the other one at the outskirts of the city with an area of 200 acres.

In common with almost all other universities, DAVV did not have a specified vision (written or unwritten), except a vague desire for advancement and dissemination of knowledge. After informal consultations with the faculty, government officials, educationists and local intelligentsia, elements of vision and associated strategy emerged on a consensus basis; though a formal statement of the mission was not drafted/documented/authorized, there was wide consensus on the change of the nature of the university from a liberal science university to a professional university (offering more and better employment opportunities for the passing students), to enhance the quantity and quality of research by securing sponsored projects from GOI agencies, direct personal approach to NET qualified candidates (by mail) to join the university as research fellows, networking with national laboratories and learned societies, using UGC unassigned grants and reforms in procedures and ordinances, related to research.

Effort was also made to obtain government support for starting new academic programmes in contemporary area of engineering sciences and strengthen existing activities (special effort was to be devoted to getting concurrence of state government for taking over the recurring expenses after 5 years), to explore self-financing and other non-conventional options for academic development and to empower and motivate schools of study and affiliated colleges towards development and excellence. The role of vice chancellor and the administration was to be mainly of a catalyst and a facilitator; the work horse for development was the faculty. The usual impediments put by the administration were to be minimized.

All schools of study were urged to develop professional employment-oriented academic programmes, on a self-financed basis; the revenue from such programmes was to be used to meet the additional expenses, including faculty, infrastructure equipment etc. and leave significant surplus for use of the school/university toward development. The University embarked on a strategy to exploit the support being offered by different departments/agencies of Govt. of India/M.P. Govt. for setting up academic/R&D programmes in emerging areas.

The university's plan for introducing employment-oriented academic programmes, was too ambitious, for the state government to support. Hence the university consciously explored the self-financing option. Although self-financed colleges in Maharashtra and Karnataka were well known, the model of a university running self-financed, as well as subsidized (usual) academic programmes did not appear to have been tried before. The rationale for self-financing is the fact that the demand for introduction of new contemporary employment-oriented academic programmes or increase in the intake for existing ones is very acute and that the demand should be considered as a means of resource generation, rather than a pressure to crush the available infrastructure.

It was realised that the university is not in a position to set up a new school of study or centre of research for each of the numerous emerging interdisciplinary areas of study and hence a mechanism had to be established for pooling the resources of different schools for interdisciplinary programmes of studies and research.

Experimentation with academic programmes of relevance, innovations for excellence, and newer modes of learning and nonconventional support for academic activities is essential for the development of a university; academic, administrative and financial empowerment at the levels of schools/institutes is also necessary for the success of the experiments. Rapid expansion should be followed by consolidation in terms of physical infrastructure, teachers, academic norms/standards and culture of research and excellence. If consolidation is overlooked, the concept rather than lousy implementation gets blamed.

The University embarked on a strategy to exploit the support being offered by different departments/agencies of Govt. of India/M.P. Govt. for setting up academic/R&D programmes in emerging areas. The eighth plan grant of UGC was utilized to augment these resources, particularly for the faculty. The prompt concurrence by the state govt. to continue the support for faculty and some recurring expenses (in the context of these emerging areas) after a period of 5 years finalized the issue and made the establishment of the new programmes in Engineering Sciences a reality.

A Blueprint of Entrepreneurship Education in India

Entrepreneurship education is a lifelong learning process, starting as early as elementary school and progressing through all levels of education, including adult education. Consortium for Entrepreneurship Education based in USA has created a framework for teachers to use in building appropriate objectives, learning activities, and assessments for their target audience. Using this framework, students will have progressively more challenging educational activities, experiences that will enable them to develop the insight needed to discover and create Entrepreneurial opportunities. The framework helps to develop the expertise to successfully start and manage their own businesses to take advantage of these opportunities.

This framework can also be applied in Indian context as it is very much in consonance with recommendations of NKC[11]which could be tested further through empirical study. National Knowledge Commission has made concrete recommendations to foster entrepreneurship and entrepreneurship education which should form part our National Education Policy. These recommendations will reap real fruit if they are implemented in letter and spirit keeping lifelong learning framework in mind.

If India has to provide good employment opportunities to its increasing population, it will definitely have to re-design the entrepreneurial education. It is only entrepreneurs who will be able to generate employment for themselves and fellow citizens. Entrepreneurial education starting right from school days will help to develop right competencies in a sizable number of people. The entrepreneurship education has to be a continuous lifelong learning system. Collaborations between Education (including modern vocational education training/skill development), Innovation (converting ideas into wealth and employment) and Entrepreneurship should be encouraged. This can start at High school. Students should experience various facets of business ownership. At this first stage the focus is on understanding the basics of economy, the career opportunities that result, and the need to master basic skills to be successful in a free market economy. The special outcomes of this lifelong learning model would be motivation to learn and a sense of individual opportunity.

Next it can also start at 10+2level.Students should learn to speak the language of business, and see the problems from the small business owner's point of view. This is particularly needed in career and technical education. The emphasis is on beginning competencies that may be taught as an entire entrepreneurship class or included as part of other courses related to entrepreneurship. For example, cash flow problems could be used in a math class, and sales demonstrations could be part of a communications class.

It needs to be also started at under graduate level. There is so much to learn about starting and running a business it is not surprising that so many businesses have trouble. We expect future doctors to learn their profession through years of formal study, yet we have expected small business owners to learn everything by attending weekend seminars. At this stage, students can take time to explore business ideas and a variety of ways to plan the business. Although, it is still only an educational experience, students must gain a greater depth and breadth of knowledge than they may have from previous stages. This stage encourages students to create a unique business idea and carry the decision-making process through a complete business plan. The best programs enable students to actually experience the operation of a business as well. The outcome is for students to learn how it might be possible to become an entrepreneur and to practice the processes of business.

After adults have had time to gain job experience and/or further their education, many are in need of special assistance to assemble a business idea. This could start at the level of post graduate classes in special entrepreneurship institutes and MBA Colleges. Some work experience should be made prerequisite for these specialist courses. Often, business owners do not seek help until it is almost too late. A series of continuing seminars or support groups can assist the entrepreneur in recognizing potential problems and how to deal with them in a thorough and timely manner. Many colleges and continuing education programs at universities or colleges offer such seminars and workshops. They recognize that the best economic development plan is to help the community's existing businesses grow and prosper.

Entrepreneurship cannot be learnt only by chalk and talk. Shared activities outside the confines of the textbook are imperative to develop leadership and team building skills that are necessary for Entrepreneurship. It is necessary to encourage activities within educational institutions, where entrepreneurial abilities find opportunities and fertile ground to grow. In several educational institutions, student led and faculty supported activities have been able to create awareness and prepare necessary mind sets about Entrepreneurship. Examples include the Entrepreneurship and Innovation Cell at IIM Bangalore and the Entrepreneurship Cell at IIT Bombay, which engage in activities such as business plan contests, assisting start-ups and incubation centres. Initiatives such as business plan contests', instructional programmes that deal with the basic practicalities of entrepreneurship and platforms to interact with other entrepreneurs and the financial community need to be intensified and encouraged. A noteworthy development is the recent proposal to set up a School of Entrepreneurship offering undergraduate and post-graduate degrees in IIT Kharagpur. Such initiatives need to be encouraged for widespread adaptation in other educational institutions, including institutions located outside metropolitan areas. The involvement of the burgeoning NRI community and alumni networks in funding such schools must be encouraged.

A survey done by the Entrepreneurship Development Institute, India (EDII) in 2003 shows that young people are afraid to start their own business because they are not confident, not capable, and lack knowledge in starting a business. Many people have the opportunity to change jobs or become an entrepreneur if they are properly trained. The students in India are not satisfied with the hands-on support of their university in the founding process. The EE in the higher education system should, therefore, satisfy the need for entrepreneurship by selecting, motivating, training and supporting. There is no system of building entrepreneurial capabilities from school level. Presently, we do not teach entrepreneurship related skills and courses in our secondary and senior secondary schools. Present EE in India just concentrates on related courses. Moreover, the so-called entrepreneurship courses are similar to the general business courses. But general business management education has no significant influence on entrepreneurial propensity, (Hostager and Decker)[12]. The findings of a survey of business owners in India suggest that management education is not an important driver of entrepreneurial attitudes, (Gupta)[13]. There is a demand for education programs specifically designed to expand students' knowledge and experience in entrepreneurship. The contents and teaching methods have to be differentiated between entrepreneurship and traditional business courses.[14]

The Vision of an Education City: A Heaven for Entrepreneurs

An innovative initiative for quality education can be taken by the central government or the state government jointly with the corporate sector by establishing Special Educational Zones (SEZs) on the lines of Special Economic Zones in the country. The zones will be primarily dedicated to the development of higher professional educational institutions, R and D centres, state of the art laboratory/workshop/ training facilities/convention centres etc. with all supportive infrastructures. These will attract investment in new establishments and new campuses of existing institutions. The suggested scheme for setting up of Special Educational Zones in the country will not only facilitate in the development of quality education and professional learning for the students of the country, it will also help export higher education, as the SEZs will attract foreign students who will pay in foreign currency to receive the domestically generated service of education in India. These earnings may in turn be ploughed back into educational investment for further improvement in quality and expansion of facilities.

An education city may be started by provision of land and basic facilities including access and communication, near a cluster of industry and business establishment. This can be financed under public private partnership. The city will have higher education institutions, R& D establishments, industrial parks (for nascent outfits) and central facilities, sports and recreational activity, centre for life skill development etc. and people/services/shops and establishments which support the working population (including students). The law and order and municipal services inclusive of gas/electricity etc. can be provided by a committee with representatives of the resident institutions, with a government official as chairman.

More about Education City has been discussed in another Reflection.

Conclusion

Experimentation with academic programmes of relevance, innovations for excellence, and newer modes of learning and nonconventional support for academic activities is essential for the development of a university. For the success of the experiments it becomes necessary to empower the schools/institutes at academicad ministrative and financial levels. The unique strength of the university viz. many schools of study or institutes in different disciplines existing side by side should be exploited for commencement and development of interdisciplinary programmes of study, research, consultancy and extension; participation of other units (outside the university) viz. other educational institutions, research institutes, business organization, industry etc. for such activities should also be seriously explored.

In conformity with the culture of the present age of knowledge, the university should have a high profile in public relations and should have active dialogues with all other interacting systems without any controversies. In this context Industry-university relations needs to be strengthened. It has been talked in detail in another chapter. Also unreasonable assumptions should be avoided. Thus, once the freedom to change structure and conventions is realized, tremendous energy for academic entrepreneurship, lateral thinking and innovations gets released. In particular financial paralysis should not be allowed to lapse into mental paralysis.

Rapid expansion should be followed by association in terms of physical infrastructure, teachers, academic norms/standards and culture of research and excellence. If this association is overlooked, the concept rather than useless implementation gets blamed. In the end, it may be pointed out that the strategy for development depends on the place and time; with the experience of others in mind and own linking, specific strategy for development at a specific place and time may be worked out.

Specific References

1. By grave, W.D. and Hofer, C.W. (1991), "Theorizing about entrepreneurship". Entrepreneurship Theory and Practice, Vol. 16, No. 2, pp. 13-22.
2. Schumpeter, J. A. (1934),The Theory of Economic Development, Cambridge, Mass.: Harvard University Press.
3. Drucker, P. (1964), Managing for Results, Harper & Row.
4. http://ptedo.com/investment/what-is-entrepreneurship/
5. Gartner, W. B. (1990). What are we talking about when we talk about entrepreneurship? Journal of Business Venturing, 5, 15-28.
6. Shane, S. & Venkataraman, S. (2007). The Promise of Entrepreneurship as a Field of Research Entrepreneurship. Springer.
7. Shane, S. A. (2003). A general theory of entrepreneurship: The individual-opportunity nexus, Edward Elgar Pub.
8. Stevenson, H. H. & Jarillo, J. C. (1990). A paradigm of entrepreneurship: entrepreneurial management. Strategic management journal, 11, 17-27.
9. Bruyat, C. & Julien, P.-A. (2001). Defining the field of research in entrepreneurship. Journal of Business Venturing, 16, 165-180.
10. https://www.investopedia.com/ask/answers/08/origin-of-entrepreneur.asp
11. Entrepreneurship in India 2008 by National Knowledge Commission.
12. Hostager, T.J. and Decker, R.L.(1999), The effects of an entrepreneurship program on achievement motivation: A preliminary study, SBIDA, San Francisco, CA: Small Business Institute Director's Association.
13. Gupta, A. (1992), The informal education of the Indian entrepreneur, Journal of Small Business and Entrepreneurship, 9 (4).
14. https://www.researchgate.net/publication/261708555_Redesigning_entrepreneurship_Education_in_India

General References

Clayton M. Christensen., The Innovator's Dilemma (Cambridge, MA: Harvard Business School Press, 1997).

Digest of Education Statistics 2004 (Washington, DC: U.S. Department of Education, National Centre for Education Statistics, 2005). http://nces.ed.gov/programs/digest/d04/index.asp

Greg Dees, (1998), "The Meaning of 'Social Entrepreneurship" (Durham, NC: Fuqua School of Business at Duke University, 1998).www.fuqua.duke.edu/centers/case/documents/dees_SE.pdf.

Howard Stevenson et al. New Business Ventures and the Entrepreneur, 5th ed. (Boston: IrwinMcGraw-Hill, 1999).

Howard H. Stevenson and William A. Sahlman. Entrepreneurship: A Process, Not a Person. (Working paper 87- 069) (Cambridge, MA: Harvard Business School, 1987).

Martin Seligman, Learned Optimism: How to Change Your Mind and Your Life (New York: Knopf, 1991).

U.S. Census Bureau, National Estimates by Age, Sex, Race: 1900 -1979. Available online at www.census.gov/popest/archives/pre-1980/PE-11.html

https://www.oecd.org/cfe/leed/BGP_Entrepreneurship-in-Education.pdf

www.scribd.com/doc/49546575/entrepreneur.

Reflection - 4

Employability in Higher Education

The Status Today

The premise that graduation is the stepping stone to the employment market holds no good in present times with a latest report[1] finding that as many as 47 per cent graduates in India are not employable for any industry role. Their lack of knowledge of English language and cognitive skills were identified as the major obstacles to their suitability in the job market. This, again, underscores the urgent necessity of intervention at school and college levels for improving basic skills of students as well as renewing the focus on imparting vocational training along with theoretical learning.

The report, titled 'Aspiring Minds: National Employability Report',[2] is a national audit of employability of three-year Bachelor's Degree graduates. The survey included 60,000 students from colleges across India, scheduled to graduate this year. According to the report, the employability of graduates varies from as low as 2.2 per cent in roles such as corporate communications/ content development and 2.59 per cent in accounting to 15.88 per cent in sales-related jobs and 21.37 per cent for roles in the business process outsourcing (BPO/ITeS) sector. Most of the graduates (35.95 per cent) were found suitable for clerical/ secretarial roles. For an analyst's role, close to 84 per cent graduates were found to lack the right levels in cognitive ability. Ninety per cent graduates did not have the required proficiency in English communication.

Another area of concern is that many graduates with accounting and information technology backgrounds remain 'invisible' to potential recruiters since they do not belong to the top colleges usually preferred by companies. Forty-one per cent of graduates employable in accounting roles hail from colleges beyond the top 30 per cent colleges, whereas for the IT services sector this percentage is 36 per cent. This system, apart from creating economic inefficiency, also breeds unfairness to students. The report points out that an effective means to tackle is to employ a scalable certification to 'discover' the employability of students across the nation.

Only 7 per cent engineering graduates are employable according to a New Delhi-based employment solutions company, 'Aspiring Minds' who conducted an employability-focused study[3] based on 150,000 engineering students who graduated in 2013. The findings were rather shocking. As many as 97 per cent of graduating engineers want jobs either in software engineering or core engineering. However, only 3 per cent have suitable skills to be employed in software or product market, and only 7 per cent can handle core engineering tasks. According to the HRD ministry, India has 6,214 engineering and technology institutions which are enrolling 2.9 million students. Around 1.5 million engineers are released into the job market every year. But the dismal state of higher education in India ensures that they simply do not have adequate skills to be employed.

So, what can happen when such a large population of youth do not get jobs? Experts say that this may cause serious instability in the economic and social conditions in the country, along with wide scale dissatisfaction and disillusionment. Though the number of universities, colleges and programmes are going on increasing in the country, the lack of quality education persists. Profit-hungry managements, lack of skill education, resplendent corruption, focus on rote-learning methods, and shortage of faculty (both in number and quality) are the major issues plaguing higher education. Graduates are collecting their degrees despite their not being skilled enough to be a productive part of the Indian economy.

India Today got together with ***Siddarth Bharwani, Vice President at Jetking Infotrain Limited***, an IT and IMS training institute, to know more about the issues contributing to such a dismal picture. Soft skills have become very important in the present job industry, but they are routinely ignored in educational institutes."This is perhaps the trickiest issue," says Bharwani. "The lack of ability of the individual to deliver his views effectively at the interview leads to rejection of even the most brilliant candidate. This is because training institutes do not make an effort to ensure that the trainees develop their skills in a wholesome manner which can contribute towards client-handling and team communication skills."The Government of India needs to sit up and take notice of the issues that are threatening the very future and stability of our country.[4]

While the Indian higher education system has made considerable progress in terms of building capacity and enrolment in the last decade, it lags significantly in terms of global relevance and competitiveness, said a study by Federation of Indian Chambers of Commerce and Industry (FICCI) and EY. The report released at the FICCI Higher Education Summit stressed that low employability of graduates is driven by factors like out-dated curricula, shortage of quality faculty, high student-teacher ratios, lack of institutional and industry linkages and lack of autonomy to introduce new and innovative courses.

"Only a small proportion of Indian graduates are considered employable. This reflects in the fact that placement outcomes drop significantly as we move away from top tier institutions," said the report. It added that this has resulted in closing down of low level higher education institutes that are not able to deliver acceptable outcomes. In 2014, nearly 120 colleges including 94 management institutes were expected to be closed down across the country because of their inability to fill the seats. In 2012, 32 engineering and management colleges stopped admitting students. Among those that closed down were 5 engineering, 9 MBA, 14 MCA, 3 pharmacies and 1 PGDM college. The report titled 'Higher Education in India: Moving towards global relevance and competitiveness' said that low impact research output and insufficient doctoral students is a gap in the system. This is shown in the number of research papers published vis-à-vis the global peers. China and U S score significantly higher in this space.

The report also focussed on the point that there is a limited focus on entrepreneurship on campuses reflected in the fact that there are few institutes that offer programmes in entrepreneurship and have active incubation/entrepreneurship cells. The research culture is also missing in most institutions.

According to the report, global relevance and competitiveness would mean India prominently placed on the global higher education map with India as a hub for talent and a culture of research, innovation and entrepreneurship. The report showed that 3.5 billion jobs are expected to be created by 2020 and China and India are likely to drive demand by 2020. Skill intensive industries such as manufacturing and services are expected to contribute more than 90% of India's GDP by 2030. Hence, the report said that the focus of employment is expected to shift towards services and manufacturing. With respect to higher education, the report said that India is expected to produce a large number of higher education graduates in the coming years. Data showed that in 2020, an estimated 42.1 million higher education enrolments will be seen in India, as compared to 28.5 million in 2012. The FICCI-EY report has aroused concerns about a few Indian higher education institutions being globally ranked. This is inspite of the fact that, India has 33,723 higher education institutions compared to 4140 in the United States.

The United States has 97 institutes in the QS World University Rankings (Top 500) 2014/15. However, India only has 6 institutes in the list. Similarly, while the US has 102 institutes in Times Higher Education World University Rankings (Top 400) 2014, India has only 4. On one hand while a large number of Indian students are going abroad to study in foreign higher education institutions, incoming foreign students are limited in number; compared to 1,90,055 students studying in higher education institutions abroad in 2012, only 31,000 foreign students came to India. The report in its vision has said that by 2030, they aspire to have 20 plus higher educational institutes in top 200 global rankings. Further, they also aspire India to be among the top 5 in terms of research and patents, with 90% graduates readily employable.[5]

Employability: The Need of the Hour

The need of the hour is to impart certain basic knowledge and skills to our children including the 3 R's as well as ethics and some other values that are universally perceived as noble. Ideally our primary education should be oriented not only to impart such education and values but, more importantly, to kindle curiosity in the minds of children by encouraging them to question, seek the answer, interpret and then come to conclusion. Their minds should not be clouded or coloured by dogmas and instead should be left free to query and learn under tolerant and able guidance of their teachers. Secondary education should focus on finding the aptitudes and abilities of the students and gently steer them to the areas of their interest as well as develop their skills while simultaneously taking their formal education to a higher level.

University education instead of mindlessly churning out large number of graduates and post graduates every year, should cater to only such students who not only have the inclination to pursue higher education but also have the aptitude for it. The rest should be gently guided towards vocational education matching their skills. However, taking such a step will not be easy at all. It will need a transformational change in the attitudes of the society which attaches enormous value to the tags of graduate and post graduate and also tends to look down upon certain vocations. The primary requisites for reversing such attitude appear to be to bring in the concept of dignity of labour and also reduce the wide disparity in the remuneration structure for different vocations.

Today our University education is rigid and inflexible; it primarily focuses on learning by rote. This needs to change immediately and drastically. There is an urgent need for Universities to resort to creative ways of teaching aided by the technologies available today, permit different combinations of subjects and encourage liberal and free thinking. The curricula for primary, secondary and University education need to be periodically reviewed and necessary changes effected so that these remain contemporary instead of being out dated as these are today. Also, ways have to be found to narrow down the differences in the quality of education in different States, Universities, Boards and schools.

Higher education is taking on a very complex, and vital role in today's world. The role of higher education institutions has changed over time from preservers of culturally revered forms of knowledge, through producers of skilled labour associated with a manpower planning approach, to the more recent perception as the agent of social change and development. A wide range of challenges and possibilities are emerging, with political, economic and social implications. It is confronted with globalization even as it struggles to overcome the inadequacies created by colonial rule and to meet the demands of development. Perhaps the most significant challenges are associated with shifting perspectives on knowledge itself, which strongly influence the role and the responsibility of the university in the context of the society.

India acquired freedom from British colonial rule in 1947. The British were indifferent to industrialization in India, and did not provide enough facilities for technical education at very few Indian universities. To support the country's planned program of economic development through industrialization, technical education is now promoted at Indian universities. In addition, special national-level centers of excellence have been established to provide world-class education in engineering, technology, management, medicine, law, and other fields. This is complemented with a range of research institutions. Several bodies have been set up to monitor standards. As the government of a welfare state, the government of independent India takes responsibility for these provisions.

The National Policy on Education (1986) characterizes Higher Education as a 'crucial factor for survival' providing the Indian people with "an opportunity to reflect on the critical, social, economic, cultural, moral and spiritual issues." The Kothari Commission's (1964-66) five-point charter of higher education aimed at generation of new knowledge, leadership, competence building, equality and social justice, still remains as a beacon of guiding principles of our educational policies. Higher education is responsible for training future professionals to occupy strategic positions in the society and the work force. Consequently, the universities play a fundamental and decisive role in enhancing knowledge, values and skills in the students. Higher education has been allocated with the most explicit role of producing highly skilled labour and research workers to meet perceived economic needs. Today, India has the world's third-largest stock of technically and professionally trained manpower. The country has achieved impressive industrialization and modernization and developed nuclear power and space technology. Professionals and technologists educated in India are respected and in demand all over the world.

Other side of the Picture

There are no two opinions about the fact that India has one of the world's largest most qualified pools of technical manpower. Each year, India produces almost twice the number of engineers produced by the US and a little less than twice of all that Europe produces. However, the other side of the picture is that positions in different fields still remain unoccupied due to lack of suitably qualified personnel. When we look at the employability, we are far behind. Degree may once have been a passport into graduate employment; it was indicative of a level of knowledge and intellectual ability. However, as a result of organizational changes and the expansion in the numbers of graduates, this is no longer the case. Working towards a higher education qualification is the ultimate goal for any undergraduate. But university life is not just about studying but is much more beyond academics. Meeting new people and enhancing social and recreational opportunities are also part of the student experience.

For decade's lack of employment opportunities and under-employment of educated masses have been important issues in Indian labour market. But employment data as obtained from 61st round of National Sample Survey (NSS) reveal that although jobs are growing at faster rate than the population, unemployment is also growing. Industry these days is not finding 'employable work force' and at the same time the government is not able to provide jobs to the people. Similarly, many of the persons are losing their jobs or failing to be promoted due to improper work habits and attitudes rather than insufficient job skills or knowledge. Employers are looking for various types of experience. They place greatest importance on employees' attitudes and basic skills over job specific skills. Due to the effect of globalization and privatization, the modus operandi of the work places is being changed drastically, and the demand for employees with basic higher order and affective skills is growing day by day. Hence a degree is no guarantee of a job, and should only be seen as reaching 'first-base' in the recruitment process.

> .... *the fact that they have that degree basically confirms they are people who think in a certain way and have certain abilities, so the next stage is a number of key competencies.*
>
> (Personal manager, multi-national food manufacturer)

Engineering colleges are mushrooming and great number of technical graduates passes out every year from educational institutions. The predicament is that nothing is done about developing employability. The way quantity of graduates is increasing the quality is not increasing. Industry looks for multi skilled individuals depending on the business it's in. Thus, what is it that we lack in our higher education system? Of course, it is the development of the attitude for employment-the spark of individuality, the confidence, and the enthusiasm towards life and of course a living philosophy of life-that the higher education needs to inspire in the students for success in the world of work. We can say we are looking for people with Emotional Intelligence.

Employability: Demand of the World of Work

Employability refers to a person's capability of gaining initial employment, maintaining employment, and obtaining new employment if required [Hillage and Pollard].[6] Employability is a union of several skills, abilities, knowledge, competencies and capabilities that enable individuals to get employment and be successful in their professional careers. It helps them individually as well as institutionally. It also dwells at the skill sets, tool sets and mindset that is essential to execute tasks effectively and efficiently. Employability depends on the knowledge, skills and attitude of the individuals. It is a state of being employed and accomplishing the given tasks with the skills, knowledge and abilities.

> "Employability not only depends on whether one is able to fulfill the requirements of specific jobs, but also on how one stands

relative to others within a hierarchy of job seekers" [Brown and Hesketh].[7]

Thus, employability is not the same as gaining a graduate job, rather it implies something about the capacity of the graduate to function in a job and be able to move between jobs, thus remaining employable throughout their life. Both universities and students want not only to survive but to thrive, prepared to tackle the key challenges faced by the societies of today and tomorrow. The potential has to be maximized, drawing on wide-ranging strengths and honest self-appraisal, engaging effectively with surrounding environments, professions and communities.

Employability can thus be defined as:

'*a set of achievements – skills, understandings and personal attributes – that make graduates more likely to gain employment and be successful in their chosen occupations, which benefits themselves, the workforce, the community and the economy*'

Professor Mantz Yorke[8]

('*Employability in Higher Education: what it is - what it is not*', Higher Education Academy/ESECT)

These attributes are key to the success of institutions and students alike, and are encompassed in Edinburgh's statement of graduate attributes.

'Graduate attributes are the qualities, skills and understandings a university community agrees its students should develop during their time with the institution. These attributes include but go beyond the disciplinary expertise or technical knowledge that has traditionally formed the core of most university courses. They are qualities that also prepare graduates as agents of social good in an unknown future.'

These attributes are skills, abilities and dispositions that transform and enable higher education knowledge and learning and must be translated into a discipline context in order to make full sense. Employers and their representatives consistently say that, to succeed at work, most people in future must develop a range of personal and intellectual attributes beyond those traditionally made explicit in programmes of study in higher education institutions.

> We do look for communication skills. We look for someone who is a team player. We look for someone who has got the ability to put forward ideas persuasively. We like to recruit people who have good social skills; they are able to relate to other people well. Linked in with that is personality and also the ability to cope with stress.
>
> **(Partner, large law firm)**

Knight and Yorke[9] developed the idea of employability further on from skills development, to considering that there are cognitive aspects to add *"what is employability? Getting a graduate job, a consequence of 'having' key skills, a likely effect of having had good work experience, a product of skilful career planning and interview technique and/or a mix of cognitive and non-cognitive achievements and representations"*.

The need for employability skills differ from one country to another. For instance, American Society for Training and Development (ASTD) identified six categories of skills which are important to employability. They are; basic competency, communication, adaptability, developmental activities, group effectiveness and influencing others. In Malaysia, these are positive values, leadership skills, teamwork force, communicative skills and life-long learning.

In Australia employability skills are defined as "the skills required for gaining employment or establish an enterprise, but also to progress within an enterprise or expand employment capability, so as to achieve one's potential and contribute successfully to an enterprise's strategic directions." The eight employability skills are initiative and enterprise, learning, self-management, communication, teamwork, problem solving, planning and organizing and technology. American Society for Training and Development (ASTD) identified a benchmark of six skill categories important to employability. These are Basic competency (reading, writing, computation), Communication (speaking, listening) Adaptability (problem solving, creative thinking), Developmental (self-esteem, motivation and goal setting, career planning),Group

Effectiveness (interpersonal, teamwork, negotiation), Influencing (understanding organization culture, sharing leadership).[10]

Interactive & Personal Attributes

Basically the employers want interactive and personal attributes in the candidates seeking employment. The core interactive skills are communication, teamwork and interpersonal skills. These are necessary to communicate, formally and informally, with a wide range of people both internal and external to the organization; to relate to, and feel comfortable with, people at all levels in the organization as well as a range of external stakeholders, to be able to make and maintain relationships as circumstances change; work effectively in teams, often more than one team at once, and to be able to re-adjust roles from one project situation to another in an ever-shifting work situation.

Personal attributes are attitudes and abilities including intellect, knowledge, willingness and ability to learn and continue learning, ability to find things out, willingness to take risks and show initiative, flexibility and adaptability to respond, anticipate and ultimately lead change and self-skills such as self-motivation, self-confidence, self-management and self-promotion. These personal attributes are important to allow graduates to fit into the work culture, do the job, develop ideas, take initiative and responsibility and ultimately help organizations deal with change, Harvey et al.[11]

On one level the set of specified skills has not changed greatly for a quarter of a century: communication skills, numeracy, self-confidence and self-discipline, problem –solving, analysis and interpersonal skills featured alongside knowledge and intelligence in organizational graduate specifications in the 1970s, [Kelsall et al.].[12] Technological and organizational changes over 25 years have added ICT skills, team working, flexibility, and adaptability. Furthermore, 'problem-solving' has become 'creative problem-solving' and risk taking has become a key attribute. On the other hand, there is much less emphasis on knowledge and far more on willingness to continue learning.

University Education: Need for Developing Attitudinal Skills for Employment

Higher education is inextricably linked to the human resource needs of the national economy and is therefore experiencing pressure to produce employable graduates. The assumption that high-level skills are indispensable in a knowledge-based economy has led governments and other stakeholders to focus increasingly on this issue. Also, students (and parents) expect a return on their investment in that they should be able to secure appropriate employment after graduation. On the other hand, media headlines frequently refer to an increase in graduate under- and unemployment. This suggests that the transition from graduate to employee may be a difficult and complex process, influenced by a variety of factors in the labour market as well as the characteristics of graduates.

There is an urgent need of introspection by the higher education institutions as regards their role of enabling the students to build capability profile that matches the requirements of work places. Graduates with excellent academic results are unable to face interview with self-confidence; lack communication skills, and are unable to take part in a group discussion, as they are hesitant and poor in basic and affective skills. The existing higher education institutions produce some degree holders with mere knowledge and information in a particular area, but it has failed to develop general employability skills needed for an entry-level employee. The Press Release dated 2nd January 2009 of the Ministry of Labour and Employment, Government of India stated that those educated but without professional skills constitute 69% of the total unemployed, whereas out of all university graduates only a meagre 13% are employable.

Often college and university students focus so much on academics that they neglect other psychosocial aspects of their lives. These aspects include social relationships (significant others, parents, and friends), environment (students are not conscious that they need time to adapt to a new environment), physical health (students often do not exercise or practice relaxation to help relieve their academic stress and frustrations), and religion and spirituality. If students are able to also focus on these areas, they will find that they are able to manage their academic and professional responsibilities more effectively.[13]

With the diverse population of students in universities today, educators must strive to create a system that reflects and celebrates diversity and allows the students to reach high standards. Educators can create new paths to learning standards by providing more learning options for students. Understanding and acceptance of oneself is the first important principle and pre-requisite for understanding the universe as a whole. Experience has shown that human resources are the most valuable assets of any profession. It is more valuable than capital or equipment. Unfortunately, it is also the most wasted. People can be the biggest asset or the biggest liability. It is the need of the hour to build up people with character, integrity, good values and a positive attitude. Any and every University today emphasizes numerous programs, mostly academic, but these will work only when we have the right foundation and that foundation is to develop values and strength of character in our students.[14]

The university along with giving the students the academic knowledge needs to train them in important skills i.e. the attitudinal skills. The students will then be able to transform their knowledge into action. Along with the regular classes there should be some sessions on personality development whereby small group of students can be given practical intensive training in developing important skills. It is the responsibility of the universities to suitably mould the attitudes of the students so that the quality of the society is improved. Surprisingly, almost 100% of money in education goes to teach facts and figures which account for only 15% of success in work. Knowledge strategically applied translates into wisdom, ensuring success. We are drowning in information but starving for knowledge and wisdom. Education, especially higher education ought to teach the youths not only how to make a living but also how to live.

Another important point to be taken care of is that there are simple graduates from Arts and Science stream i.e. simple B.A. and B.Sc. students. After completing their graduation, these students have nowhere to go because firstly they lack core skills to make their place in the world of work and secondly they are confused youth who are not goal oriented. Our unemployed engineers and students from management courses also need serious support to make their standing. Here it becomes important for the university, industry/business to start some bridge courses to prepare these graduates for the market. It will definitely be good if such courses are supported by the government.

Along with these bridge courses the higher education institutes should start diploma and certificate courses in soft skills like speaking English, working Hindi, communication skills, computer literacy etc. In fact there should be a soft skill lab in every university and college and Higher Education Institutions that will help to build these skills in students so that they can ultimately prepare themselves to establish in the world of work. In fact it should be the responsibility of every department to start such courses along with the normal academic courses so that a student is prepared to face interviews when ultimately he/she cracks competitions and has to face interviews. An example can be the active participation of Teacher Education/Training Departments in the country. These teacher training courses can alongside provide short courses in English speaking to students who are weak in language so that when they get placement they are confident enough to build their future. The university degree should not be considered complete without a certificate and training in soft skills.

The students should get work experience in the campus itself by engaging them in part time jobs. Summer placement of students can be planned in small and large scale establishments so that they can get hands-on-experience. They can also undertake cooperative projects in summer. There are a number of students who get an opportunity to work abroad but they lack either language or soft skills to settle in a new country. In this respect students should be given courses like in Spanish language so that it becomes easy for them to communicate in Spanish, which is spoken by large number of people over the world and experts are not available in the same proportion. Therefore, it becomes important to prepare students in this language.

They should be oriented in job opportunities abroad and should be prepared for those jobs. They should be helped to develop skills to face interviews for government jobs which will also help them to qualify for private jobs. There is also an immense need to infuse the spirit of entrepreneurship in our students- the attitude of taking risks. The basic concept of entrepreneurship entails an effective and deliberate inner urge to take risk in terms of uncertainties and an intuition. The common definition for an entrepreneur is a person, who organizes, manages, and takes the risk of running a business or enterprise. The entrepreneurs perform vital function in economic development of a nation. They have been referred to as the human agents needed to mobilize capital, to exploit natural resources, too often develop innovative products or concepts, to create markets and to carry on business. It may be construed that the entrepreneurial contribution spells the difference between prosperity and poverty among nations.

The importance of entrepreneurs to progress cannot be more succinctly expressed than the statement – no entrepreneur, no development. The inactivity or scarcity of entrepreneurs has for sometimes been the factor seen by many Asian countries as a major hindrance to economic development. The availability of abundant natural resources, skilled and unskilled labour, and capital has not proven itself sufficient enough to result in a surge of entrepreneurial zeal among the people. One of the important inputs in any economic development of a country is entrepreneurship. More the entrepreneurship activities, better the development. Entrepreneurship is the life blood of any economy and it applies more to a developing economy like India. This attitude of entrepreneurship has to be inculcated in the graduates and undergraduates so that after completing their education they are not roaming like vagabonds to find job but instead they develop themselves as job givers and as successful entrepreneurs. More about entrepreneurship has been discussed in another chapter.

In a rapidly changing world, graduates need to be lifelong *learners*. The primary role of higher education is increasingly to transform students by *enhancing* their knowledge, skills, attitudes and abilities while simultaneously *empowering* them as lifelong critical, reflective learners.

A reflection on Entrepreneurship in Universities has been discussed in a separate chapter.

Suggestions for developing Employability

The following suggestions if incorporated by our higher education institutions can definitely prove to be a milestone in making our graduates more employable.

1. *Incorporating cultivation of general employability into the curricula and teaching*

Every individual has several abilities and potentialities. Employability can be divided into general abilities and professional abilities. At present, institutions of higher learning are often only concerned about cultivation of professional abilities through study of professional courses and professional practice ignoring the cultivation of general abilities. In higher education, by employability, people usually think of professional practice and training of professional skills. Given the growing trend towards diverse and flexible demand for personnel in the labor market, university students must strengthen their general abilities. British higher education policy proposes that opportunity of developing students' general abilities shall be provided in the general curricula and meanwhile students shall be allowed to understand how general abilities are included in curricula in the course description and the development of students' employability shall be recorded in their learning records (Tariq, Scott, Cochrane, Lee, & Ryles.[15]

Thus, it is important that development and training of graduates in general attitudinal skills and abilities should be incorporated in the general curricula and teaching of the higher education institutions so that it becomes a part and parcel of the students education.

2. *Increasing the proportion of practical teaching*

Learning from practical experience is the most effective way to build employability. Therefore, it would be better to "allow students to have the opportunity to practice these core employability skills in a real, if not possible then simulated, work environment throughout degree courses" Crebert et al.[16] Through practical experience, students can confirm the relation of what they learn in classroom and the reality, make self-assessment and develop personality characteristics conducive to work; develop specific communication and interaction skills to encourage their motivation of learning and apply theories to real work to realize that academic success is not a sufficient condition for employment success.

The Ministry of Education introduced a series of policies in 2009 to promote employment of university students, which clearly states:

"make great efforts to organize practice aiming at promoting employment to ensure that all graduates can take part in practical activities before graduation and enhance the workplace adaptability of graduates". Therefore, in the process of personnel training, institutions of higher learning shall increase input at the link of practical teaching and practice and increase the proportion of this part in the evaluation system for university students. Besides, it is also very important to guide teachers to pay attention to practical teaching through policies.

3. Establishing a scientific assessment and follow-up mechanism for the employability of university students

When formulating student-training programs, institutions of higher learning need to comprehensively research the knowledge, skills and attitudes needed by students to meet employment requirements, design employability models for university students majoring in various disciplines that not only conform to the law of development of the discipline, but also meet the market demand through research and transform training objectives to competency standards based on the classification system of general and professional abilities. The result of training shall be measured against the fulfillment of competency standards. By designing the students' employability measurement indicator system based on the university students' employability model and through development of application tools, on the one hand, we can help institutions of higher learning evaluate and track the status of the employability of university students to constantly adjust the direction and method of teaching; on the other hand, we can enable university standards to analyse their own advantages and disadvantages in the process of obtaining employment to help match students with employers and vice versa.

4. Evaluating the teaching quality of institutions of higher learning through the status of graduates' employability

As the difficulty of finding employment for university graduates become increasingly prominent, the employment status of graduates already reflects the teaching quality and training result of the institute to some extent. Although the employment status of graduates are influenced by many factors, students' employability is a major issue that cannot be ignored, attention should be paid to studying the status of graduates' employability in the process of evaluating the teaching quality of institutions of higher learning. The world's famous research companies My COS and Gallup used employability as an indicator to evaluate the teaching quality of institutions of higher learning in their *"2007 Report on the Employment of Chinese University Graduates"* and published the "ranking list of employability of universities" for two consecutive years (2007 and 2008) according to the data of survey on this year's graduates half a year after their graduation, producing a tremendous influence on institutions of higher learning and society. Emergence of the ranking list shows the social concern about employment of university graduates and also reflects the strong demand of the market for cultivation of the employability of university students, thus promoting reform of the personnel training model of higher education in a direction conducive to enhancing the employability of students.

Thus finally, any and every University should:

- Modify admission criteria to take account of leadership and other dimensions of the whole student.
- Nurture the individual student to ensure highest probability of success. We must assume responsibility for the success of our students.
- Increase opportunities for all students to develop academic and social experience that facilitate academic success and involvement in the life of the institution. Students and faculty should be brought into more frequent and productive interaction. The number of small classes for undergraduates should be doubled so that more practical intensive training in attitudinal development can be easily imparted.
- All students should have readily available opportunities for academic and attitudinal enrichment experiences appropriate to their educational goals. A systematic approach and infrastructure needs to be developed to facilitate opportunities for all students to have enrichment experiences, such as expanded honours courses, study-abroad experiences, interdisciplinary curricula, cooperative education, experiences

on managing human relations and research opportunities. They should be given opportunities to apply the skills learnt in their real life.

- Evaluation should be continuous and academic offerings and curricula should be adjusted to keep them relevant and strong.
- Efforts should be made for determination of attitude, professional suitability and potential by psychological tests.
- Sensitize faculty and others to the employability needs of students.

Conclusion

It would be wise to conclude with the statement of Peter Hawkins **"To be employed is to be at risk, to be employable is to be secure."** After a detailed analysis of what is the actual meaning of being employable, it becomes easier to remark that mere academic abilities alone in our graduates will not be adequate. What is essential is something beyond academic domain such as emotional intelligence, communication skills, problem-solving skills, human relation skills, team spirit and true leadership quality, which are known as employability skills. When applicants possess these skills then it becomes easier for employers to train other technical skills easily. Thus, both educational institutions and industry should work together for enhancing employability skills as it is rightly said that we need to clap with both hands to get effective results. At individual level also a student should work on himself/herself as far as his/her personality characteristics are concerned. They should look for opportunities so that they can prepare themselves to face interviews confidently. Developing core competencies which will help them to ultimately achieve success in their career and life is very important for the students in the modern times.

The mission of higher education is multi-layered and includes both training of creative personnel who can start innovative science of humanity in future and training of a large number of outstanding application-oriented personnel for the current socio and economic development. Therefore, establishing a higher education system in which teaching and research run parallel to vocational and professional training with the help of intensive training in attitudinal development, will definitely help in forming balance personalities who will be not only academically sound but also willevelop the skills that will help them live a much more satisfied and successful life and through which they will be able to actualize their potentialities in real sense.

Mantz Yorke asserts that *'the best that can realistically be achieved may be for higher education to facilitate the development in students of the understandings, skills and attributes that will help them to make a success of their careers'.*

Specific References

1. Raktima Bose JUNE 26, 2013 https://www.thehindu.com/news/cities/delhi/nearly-47-per-cent-graduates-in-india-unemployable-says-report/article4850167.ece
2. https://www.aspiringminds.com/research-reports
3. https://www.aspiringminds.com/sites/default/files/National%20Employability%20Report%20-%20Engineers%20Annual%20Report%202016.pdf
4. https://www.indiatoday.in/education-today/featurephilia/story/engineering-employment-problems-329022-2016-07-13
5. M Saraswathy |https://www.business-standard.com/article/management/employability-of-graduates-big-concern-says-ficci-ey-report-114111301099_1.html
6. Hillage, J. & Pollard, E. (1998) Employability: developing a framework for policy analysis, DfEE Research Briefing No. 85. London, DfEE.
7. Brown P, Hesketh A (2004). The Mismanagement of Talent: Employability and Jobs in the Knowledge Economy. Oxford: Oxford University Press.
8. Yorke, M. (2004). Employability in higher education: what it is – what it is not? P.11 HEA UK ESECT.
9. Knight, P., &Yorke, M. (2004). Learning, curriculum, and employability in higher education. London: Routledge.
10. http://profmsr.blogspot.com/2010/04/employability-skills-profmsrao.html#ixzz5NA3CqGMY
11. Harvey, L. & Knight, P.T. (1996). *Transforming Higher Education*. Buckingham: Society for Research into Higher Education (SRHE) and Open University Press.
12. Kelsall, R.K., Poole, A. & Kuhn, A. (1972). Graduates: The Sociology of Elite. London: Methuen.

13. Soni, R.(2005).Higher Education Beyond Academics, *University News*: A Weekly Journal of Higher Education, 43 (44), October 31- Nov. 06.

14. Soni, R. (2011). *Higher Education: an Introduction*, New Delhi: Anamaya Publications.

15. Tariq, V., Scott, E., Cochrane, A., Lee, M., & Ryles, L. (2004). Auditing and mapping key skills within university curricula. Quality Assurance in Education, 12(2), 70-81. http://dx.doi.org/ 10.1108/09684880410536440

16. Crebert, G., Bates, M., Bell, B., Patrick, C-J. & Cragnolini, V. (2004). Developing Generic Skills at University, during Work Placement and in Employment: Graduates' Perceptions. Higher Education Research and Development, 23(2), 147-165.

General References

Barnett, R. (2000). *Realizing the University in an Age of Super complex*ity, Ballmoor, UK: SRHE and Open University Press.

Bowden, J., Hart, G., King, B., Trigwell, K., & Watts, O. (2000).*Generic capabilities of ATN university graduates*, Canberra: Australian Government Department of Education, Training and Youth Affairs.

Brown, P., Hesketh, A. and Williams, S. (2002) Employability in a knowledge-driven economy. In Knight, P. (compiler) Notes from the 13th June 2002 'Skills plus' conference, Innovation in education for employability held at Manchester Metropolitan University.

Coate, K., Court, S., Gillon, E., Morley, L., & Williams, G. (2000). Academic and Academic Related Staff Involvement in the Local, Regional and National Economy. London: Association of University Teachers.

Drucker, P. (1993) Post-Capitalist Society, London: HarperCollins.

Edwards, G. *Connecting PDP to Employer Needs and the World of Work*. Higher Education Academy.

Harvey, L., Locke, W., & Morey, A. (2002). Enhancing Employability, Recognizing Diversity. London: Universities UK.

Lam, D., (2007). "The demography of youth in developing countries and its economic implications", *World Bank Policy Research Working Paper 4022*, included in world development report.

Martin Seligman, Learned Optimism: How to Change Your Mind and Your Life (New York: Knopf, 1991).Morley, L. (2001). Producing New Workers: Quality, Equality and Employability in Higher Education.*Quality in Higher Education*, 7(2), 131-138.

OECD. Competencies for the Knowledge Economy, Paris: OECD.2001.

Ray, S. and Chand, R., *Socio-Economic Dimensions of Unemployment in India*, NSSO, New Delhi.

Shukla, R., (2006). *India Science Report*, National Council for Applied Economic Research.

Skills Task Force (STF) (1998).*Towards a National Skills Agenda: First Report of the National Skills Task Force*. Sudbury, Suffolk: DFEE Publications.

World Youth Report, United Nations, 2003.

Watts, A.G. *Career Development Learning and Employability* (2006) – Higher Education Academy Learning and Employability Series Two.

http://profmsr.blogspot.com/2010/04/employability-skills profmsrao.html#ixzz1HRGR5vri

Reflection - 5

Higher Education beyond Academics: Education Plus

Introduction

Pandit Jawahar Lal Nehru (1947) in his convocation address at the University of Allahabad summed up the basic objectives of the university and its role in national life as: '*A University stands for humanism, for tolerance, for reason for the adventure of ideas and for the search of truth. It stands for the onward march of the human race towards even higher objectives. If the Universities discharge their duties adequately, then it is well with the nation and the people.*' Nehru highlighted the basic truth that the universities have a crucial part to play in the life, welfare and strength of a nation. Their principal object is to deepen man's understanding of the universe and of himself: in body, mind and spirit, to disseminate this understanding throughout society and to apply it in the service of mankind.

There are many traits, skills, attitudes, values and aspects of knowledge, which are necessary for success in life, entry in a profession at a suitable level and professional progress, but are acquired to a limited extent, during conventional studies in a college or in a university; such characteristics may be called Education Plus. These skills include Communication Skills, through Hindi, English and a regional language; Logical Skills; Numerical Skills; Creative skills, General Awareness, Computer skills, Entrepreneurial skills; stress management and values cum ethics.

The extent to which skills get acquired during studies depend on the quality of the educational institution, facilities and environment at home, knowledge/skills/attitudes in the family, friends and neighborhood, and availability of counseling and guidance by professionals and elders. The difference between level of Education Plus in students, from metropolitan cities, other cities and rural areas is too significant to be missed even by a casual observer. Since Educational Plus is essential for excellence in life and profession and is not normally acquired during conventional education, it is essential that a conscious programme raises the level of Education Plus among students. Such a programme is also bound to raise the curricular scholastic level and the self-confidence of the participants and develop their personality.

Appreciation

The success of a programme of this nature requires an appreciation of the programme by the prospective participants (students), parents, leaders of community, employers, teachers, administrators, mass media, and the public in general. The programme must be acceptable to the public at large, particularly if significant state funding is called for; the opinion leaders and mass media can play a key role to this end. The effectiveness of the programme depends on the eagerness of participation by the youth, which implies a high degree of motivation. The teachers undertaking various components of the programme have also to be motivated enough to take up this assignment, which may not be much in line of their specialization and current interest; he may possibly be emphasizing the challenges in his financial incentives. This mission should be attractive to disadvantaged sections of society, if presented in an effective manner.

Aims of Higher Education beyond Academics

Why join a University?

A student often thinks, 'why go to a University - what can it offer me?' People from all ages and backgrounds have decided to enter higher education, and for a variety of reasons. Although the decision to enter higher education is a very individual one, but many students enter university to get a suitable job, experience the lifestyle and for meeting new people. University is about more than what is taught within the walls of a classroom. It is about getting involved and becoming a part of campus life. From joining a student organization to volunteering in the community, leadership skills are a necessity. The personal development and growth that a student experiences will make him/her more organized, confident, and capable of handling the responsibilities of college and career. He/she will greatly enhance the ability to work in a more effective and efficient manner with a broader panorama of people.

Institutions may be created by individuals but the creators cannot regulate its growth as the institutions get their own life and they proceed according to that. All that one can do from outside is to try and have such people as can give the correct guidance. By guidance is meant not forcing any ideology or restricting the conduct in a particular way. Guidance is to see how the personality of the individual is allowed to grow in its own way. Whether it is one mile away or a thousand miles away, going to a university can be a very exciting yet anxious time, especially for first-year students. Unfortunately, experience has taught us that many first-year students do not realize that going away to college requires a shedding of skin or a transformation from their previous high school mentality and lifestyle. The situations and decision-making that students experience in college, whether academic or personal, are often radically different than the experience in high school, making it safe to conclude that a first-year student is still, at least to start with, in the mindset of a high school student.

Often college students focus so much on academics that they neglect other physical and psychosocial aspects of their lives. These aspects include social relationships (significant others, parents, family and friends), community, environment (students are not conscious that they need time to adapt to a new environment), physical health (students often do not exercise or practice relaxation to help relieve their academic stress and frustrations). Religion and spirituality (students may not focus on gaining support from their pastor, minister, or place of worship) help students to manage their academic responsibilities more effectively.

Education plus: Need of the Day

It's not enough to keep saying that our goal is "academic excellence," as though that means something sufficiently neutral and obvious to everyone. We need to replace the word "academic" with new words for what we're after—with a language that carries a different set of connotations. If habits of mind are the goal, then things other than the academic disciplines themselves can serve as subject matter. Working towards a higher educational qualification is the ultimate goal for any undergraduate. But university life is not just about studying. Meeting new people and enhancing your social and recreational opportunities are also part of the student experience.[1]

A high quality of life for students is a clear demonstration of our commitment to educational opportunities. Many factors impact the quality of student life. An excellent library, state-of-the-art information technology, appropriate laboratories and classrooms all affect the academic dimension of student life. One of the chief determinants of the quality of student life is the degree of interaction between faculty and students. Communion of faculty and students is the core of learning. Skilled teachers intensify learning by providing authentic instruction and meaningful assignments while holding high expectations for all students. Such assignments deal with the significant concepts of discipline, incorporate higher-order thinking skills, are connected to the "real world," and allow substantial time for discussion and idea sharing among students. [Peterson].[2]

With the diverse population of students in universities today, educators must strive to create a system that reflects and celebrates diversity and allows the students to reach high standards. Educators can create new paths to learning standards by providing more learning options for students.

The Delivery System

Formal

Education Plus can be best given as an integral part of structured learning in universities/colleges and possibly schools on mandatory or voluntary basis. The foundation course at bachelor's level may be reorganized to include many components of Education Plus. Readings from contemporary magazines/newspapers can substitute conventional texts and help comprehension skills as well as awareness. Certificate or non-credit programmes for the other skills/values/aptitude can also be launched.

Informal

For youth, who have finished college education an accelerated time frame can be useful. The present practice of coaching by private agencies and the government aiming at a specific examination is of limited usefulness. The acquisition of Education Plus should be a long term; it is not a life long process. The informal programme should be of a modular nature, with counseling facilities. The participants can choose one or more modules of interest and pursue it at a pace of their choice. The modules may also be offered by the institution or private agencies for students pursuing a degree course.[3]

Financing Education Plus

The progarmme of Education Plus viz. providing education beyond academics can be successful if and only if well financed. Some of the sources which can be worked upon are:

1. **Government:** At present the government is offering free coaching for SC, ST and OBC and minority communities for specific examinations, the scope of activity may be extended to Education plus for a long period and inclusion of general category youth at marginal cost.
2. **Community Participation:** The community in general is unlikely to financially support such a programme. However, sections of community (like minorities, OBC) may be persuaded to support Education Plus programme for Youth belonging to that community.
3. **Private Initiative:** The youth and their parents are willing to pay high fees for any programme, which enhances the chances of employment at a level considered satisfactory by the youth. Education Plus is a long term investment for the youth and good business for the entrepreneurs. Coaching for

competitive examination is a small portion of the field of Education Plus.

4. **Aid from Abroad:** There are some organizations of non-resident Indians, who may offer assistance on general community basis in terms of expertise and finance. The acceptance and utilization of this assistance has to be examined in the context that it should not make the programme dependent on foreign aid.

Skill Development

"Skilling is building better India. If we have to move India towards development then Skill Development should be our mission."

Shri Narendra Modi, Prime Minister of India

Red Fort, Delhi 15th August 2014

Skill India is a campaign launched by Prime Minister Narendra Modi on 15 July 2015 which aims to train over 40 crore people in India in different skills by 2022. It includes various initiatives of the government like "National Skill Development Mission", "National Policy for Skill Development and Entrepreneurship, 2015", "Pradhan Mantri Kaushal Vikas Yojana (PMKVY)" and the "Skill Loan scheme".

The National Skill Development Corporation India (NSDC) was setup as a one of its kind, Public Private Partnership Company with the primary mandate of catalyzing the skills landscape in India. It is based on the following pillars:

1. Create large and good quality vocational institute.
2. Reduce risk by providing patient capital. Including grants and equity.
3. To enable the creation and sustainability of support systems required for skill development. This includes the Industry led Sector Skill Councils.

Pradhan Mantri Kaushal Vikas Yojana (PMKVY) is the flagship scheme of the Ministry of Skill Development & Entrepreneurship (MSDE). The objective of this Skill Certification Scheme is to enable a large number of Indian youth to take up industry-relevant skill training that will help them in securing a better livelihood. Individuals with prior learning experience or skills will also be assessed and certified under Recognition of Prior Learning (RPL). Under this Scheme, Training and Assessment fees are completely paid by the Government.

Key Components of the Scheme

1. *Short Term Training*

The Short Term Training imparted at PMKVY Training Centres (TCs) is expected to benefit candidates of Indian nationality who are either school/college dropouts or unemployed. Apart from providing training according to the National Skills Qualification Framework (NSQF), TCs shall also impart training in Soft Skills, Entrepreneurship, Financial and Digital Literacy. Duration of the training varies per job role, ranging between 150 and 300 hours. Upon successful completion of their assessment, candidates shall be provided placement assistance by Training Partners (TPs). Under PMKVY, the entire training and assessment fees are paid by the Government. Pay outs shall be provided to the TPs in alignment with the Common Norms. Trainings imparted under the Short Term Training component of the Scheme shall be NSQF Level 5 and below.

2. *Recognition of Prior Learning*

Individuals with prior learning experience or skills shall be assessed and certified under the Recognition of Prior Learning (RPL) component of the Scheme. RPL aims to align the competencies of the unregulated workforce of the country to the NSQF. Project Implementing Agencies (PIAs), such as Sector Skill Councils (SSCs) or any other agencies designated by MSDE/NSDC, shall be incentivized to implement RPL projects in any of the three Project Types (RPL Camps, RPL at Employers Premises and RPL centres). To address knowledge gaps, PIAs may offer Bridge Courses to RPL candidates.

3. *Special Projects*

The Special Projects component of PMKVY envisages the creation of a platform that will facilitate trainings in special areas and/or premises of Government bodies, Corporates or Industry bodies, and trainings in special job roles not defined under the available Qualification Packs

(QPs)/National Occupational Standards (NOSs). Special Projects are projects that require some deviation from the terms and conditions of Short Term Training under PMKVY for any stakeholder. A proposing stakeholder can be Government Institutions of Central and State Government(s)/Autonomous Body/Statutory Body or any other equivalent body or corporates who desire to provide training to candidates.

4. *Kaushal and Rozgar Mela*

Social and community mobilisation is extremely critical for the success of PMKVY. Active participation of the community ensures transparency and accountability, and helps in leveraging the cumulative knowledge of the community for better functioning. In line with this, PMKVY assigns special importance to the involvement of the target beneficiaries through a defined mobilisation process. TPs shall conduct Kaushal and Rozgar Melas every six months with press/media coverage; they are also required to participate actively in National Career Service Melas and on-ground activities.

5. *Placement Guidelines*

PMKVY envisages linking the aptitude, aspiration, and knowledge of the skilled workforce it creates with employment opportunities and demands in the market. Every effort thereby needs to be made by the PMKVY TCs to provide placement opportunities to candidates, trained and certified under the Scheme. TPs shall also provide support to entrepreneurship development.

6. *Monitoring Guidelines*

To ensure that high standards of quality are maintained by PMKVY TCs, NSDC and empaneled Inspection Agencies shall use various methodologies, such as self-audit reporting, call validations, surprise visits, and monitoring through the Skills Development Management System (SDMS). These methodologies shall be enhanced with the engagement of latest technologies.

The scheme will be implemented through the National Skill Development Corporation (NSDC).[4]

Many aspects of Skill development may not be of interest to Universities but some areas are certainly within university interest and competence. The University should seek out such opportunities. The university can have a unit or some allotted time for students. During graduation level itself we should teach students these skills.

Apart from the above Skill development programme offered by the Government of India, the educational institutions should give importance in developing the following skills in students:

Communication Skills

Good communication skills are essential for survival in self-employment, getting a job and retaining it or progress in the profession. The employer has a chance to explore the knowledge, talent and skills of a person only when a minimum level of communication gets established; higher the level of communication, better is the basis for mutual association; Self-employment implies contacts to be fruitful which is effective communication. In the same way the progress of an individual is to a great extent determined by the impression he creates on others and his ability of persuasion; all these characteristics depend on the level of communication.

Logical Skills

These are essential for rational decision making and hence many employers insist on an incumbent, possessing these in an adequate measure; for assessment of logical skills, tests are usually administered. Every person has some inherent logical skills, which can be improved by training; the training can comprise of few lectures and many exercises. Training in logical skills can also take out the fear of unknown from those, who are first exposed to tests in logical skills.

Numerical Skills

Appreciation of quantitative aspects of a situation and the ability to sort out the effect of change in one or more parameters is an essential requirement in decision making. The ability to see trends in a mass of data and select significant parameters is extremely desirable. Understanding of data, presented graphically in a variety of ways and corresponding presentation is also an important aspect of numerical skills.

Comprehension Skills

The comprehension of a written document or an oral presentation and recognition of salient points is very important in any profession and hence the corresponding skills are useful to do well in any profession.

Creative Skills

Creativity is the ability to think non-conventionally and come up with new ideas, leading to new products, methodologies and correlation. A highly disciplined mind, dedicated to think and act according to the book is unlikely to be creative, unless so trained.

General Awareness

All professions are affected by the world around them and hence require that the professionals have general awareness and appreciation of the world around them; this also helps them to recognize or seek out opportunities for organizations and individuals. General awareness is best acquired by observation, exposure and study over a long period of time and also by living in an enlightened environment. Hence it is natural to find a large variance in the level of awareness between the privileged class, characterized by access to a variety of sources of informal learning, an enlightened environment, a good school and bright friends and others, who do not have these facilities to a significant extent.

Wherever required general awareness can be increased by structured, formal and guided as well as frequent exposure to knowledgeable persons from different backgrounds; a habit of reading newspapers, magazines, selected audio visual programmes and travel/ visits also help.

Computer and Information Technology Skills

Computers have penetrated personal and professionals, to an extent that a professional is required to be not only a computer literate but rather proficient in use of computers; computer applications are too numerous, diverse and useful to be enumerated here. Suffice to say that not only professional but any student has to be soon proficient in computers, at least in applications to his discipline and work.

Entrepreneurial Skills

Enterprise is the most desirable characteristics which a nation, community or an individual needs for progress and development. Despite some individuals and communities, who have displayed remarkable enterprise, as a nation we have failed to be entrepreneurial in attitude. Such an attitude can be cultivated by study of success stories in enterprise, in India and abroad and developing entrepreneurs into role models for the younger generation. Entrepreneurial skills are to some extent inherent in an individual, but can be cultivated by text, simulated exercises and exposure to the real world.

Personality Development: University's primary function

Our first cause, that without which all others lose purpose, is the student. Our culture should value, above all else, the students and the educational opportunities afforded them, especially through excellence in teaching. Our need to be responsive to changing realities as well as the need for interdisciplinary work to solve complex problems leads to new thinking about curricula. Curricula must be in tune with the forces at work in the world, the needs of students, and the expert understanding of faculty. The changes required may force us to rethink the nature of degree programs and to balance disciplinary traditions with other forces. We should aim to provide a university climate that is learner-centered, emphasize academic rigor and high expectations of students, faculty, and staff; encourage involvement in the life of the institution beyond the classroom; foster an environment of caring and concern, which promotes success and leadership development for all students.

Rabindranath Tagore on the establishment of Vishva Bharati University at Shanti Niketan in early 20's wanted to link education with nature and emphasized the development of personality of an individual in totality. If we study the political systems of the developing countries, we observe that these countries have all types of governances, such as democracy, communism, monarchy and military. But in all these countries we observe the same kind of problems viz. poverty, illiteracy, unemployment, disease and crime. Hence, it is clear that only mental empowering can change the society and the world and not the system of governance. Human beings possess four dimensions of power: physical, mental, intellectual and spiritual. Good quality higher education must empower a person in all the four dimensions. With this backdrop, Swami Vivekananda said:

> "We want that education by which character is formed, strength of mind is increased, the intellect is expanded and by which one can stand on one's own feet."

Understanding and acceptance of oneself is the first important principle and pre-requisite for understanding the universe as a whole. Experience has shown that human resources are the most valuable assets of any profession. It is more valuable than capital or equipment. Unfortunately, it is also the most wasted. People can be the biggest asset or the biggest liability. It is the need of the hour to build up people with character, integrity, good values and a positive attitude. Any and every University today emphasizes numerous programs, mostly academic, but these will work only when we have the right foundation.

According to Dr. William James of Harvard University, the greatest discovery of this generation is that human beings can alter their lives by altering their attitudes of mind. Most of our attitude is established during our formative years. It is the responsibility of the universities to suitably mould the attitudes of the students so that the quality of the society is improved. Surprisingly, almost 100% of money in education go to teach facts and figures which account for only 15% of success in work. Knowledge strategically applied translates into wisdom, ensuring success. We are drowning in information but starving for knowledge and wisdom. Education, especially higher education ought to teach the youth not only how to make a living but also as to how to live. For holistic personality development, apart from academics all these are needed: Sports, Education in Human values, yoga, meditation, NSS, NCC, etc.

Learning is acquiring necessary knowledge and skills for better performance. A commission appointed by UNESCO[5] has recommended four pillars of learning.

1. Learning to know

2. Learning to do
3. Learning to be
4. Learning to live and work together

Learning is at the central core of an educational system. The quality of the society is enhanced when the quality of the individuals is enhanced. Universities as at present, place more emphasis on the first two pillars of learning. Unless the university system strengthens the last two pillars of learning, the learning society system becomes unstable.

The Universities should strengthen the following desirable attributes of the 21st century learners so that the 21st century society is enriched:

1. A positive attitude in life
2. Learnability: learning to learn, on one's own
3. Zeal for life-long learning
4. Communication skills
5. Ability to get knowledge from other disciplines
6. Ability to work in a team
7. Creative skills
8. Integrative skills
9. International outlook
10. Ability to employ information technology

Preparing for life with a scientific frame of mind is more essential than preparing for examination. For a country to grow meaningfully and in a sustainable way, the university systems and colleges have to become centers of excellence where the best minds apply themselves to the task of moulding India's coming generation.[6]

Mental Health and Hygiene for University Students

The term 'mental health problems' is one that incorporates a range of experiences and situations. Mental health might usefully be viewed as a continuum of experience, from mental well-being through to a severe and enduring mental illness. We all experience changes in our mental health state influenced by social, personal, financial and other factors. Major life events such as a close bereavement, or leaving home, can impact significantly on how we feel about ourselves, for example, leading to depression and anxiety. Our mental well-being is an issue for all of us to consider all the time, as we might consider our physical well-being. Given support and information people experiencing mental health problems can make positive changes and improvements.

An increasing number of students at University are experiencing mental health problems that impact not only on their academic work, but also on all other aspects of their University life. Mental health problems not only have implications for the student involved, but often also for those around them: friends, colleagues, staff and family. Generally the university boys and girls today lack mental peace because of the following psychological problems for which they need guidance and support:

1. Feeling of insecurity as a result of future unemployment
2. Stress, anxiety and hypertension
3. Aggression, frustration and alienation

Students have an increasing need for psychological services and related resources; hence there is an urgency of expansion of these services. Such services include providing information about what mental health problems are, how to recognize when someone is struggling with them, and the range of support services within the University that can provide consultation, advice and more direct involvement to best support the students and those around them. The University-community interaction in health sector is very crucial. The community people particularly youth and women are in reproductive and productive age group; they could be mobilized through health and educational intervention. Health issues particularly adolescent-health and reproductive health are their immediate concern. They need behavioral change by communication on population and Health issues.[7]

The UGC under its policy frame of Xth Plan[8] has recognized university based and the community based counseling services. Under the community based services as peer educators, after proper financing and orientation, visit the community and provide the following services:

1. Proper Information and Communication on Food/ Nutrition

2. Adolescent physical, social and mental growth
3. Health needs of the girl child, street children and the marginalized children
4. Counseling on family welfare issues and on life skills issues
5. Counseling on pre and post test HIV AIDS counseling

A review of some of the researches conducted abroad has emphasized the need and importance of mental health services in schools, colleges and universities. A study conducted in University of Michigan by Megivern, Mary Deborah (2001) on *Educational functioning and college integration of students with mental illness: Examining the roles of psychiatric symptomatology and Mental Health service use* showed that college students with Mental illness were capable of academic performance equivalent to that of students without mental health problems. However, the academic and social aspects of college were taxing for these students, particularly if they were not receiving effective mental health services. Results indicated the need for better processes for assisting students experiencing serious symptoms on campus. Suggestions included a better referral system and improved coordination between Higher Education Mental health resources and the community based mental health system.[9]

Wagner and Kari Lynn at Spalding University conducted another study *"A program evaluation model for the mental health counseling component of the Youth services centers within Jefferson County, Louisville, Kentucky"* in the year 2002. The underlying conceptualization for the evaluation based upon a review of the literature, was that school based Mental Health counselors provide a social support to at-risk students, thereby increasing the students' ability to deal with life stressors resulting in an increased capacity for academic achievement.

Another study *"An analysis of differences between successful and unsuccessful high risk university students"* by Janet in the University of Memphis in 1995, emphasized the need for careful monitoring of students with regard to their study habits, attributions for success, participation in on-campus activities because these factors seem to impact academic success. It has long been the primary purpose of the remedial and developmental programmes in Higher Education to increase the probability of academic success for high- risk students.

Thus, it is established that there is an urgent need to provide mental health services in every university institution to help the young girls and boys to develop a positive attitude that contributes to 85% of success in an individual's life. It will help them develop numerous skills and will contribute in providing them sufficient knowledge and skill to deal with the stressors in life.

Counselling and Psychological support in the University campus

In the yester years, educational counseling was not seen as an activity independent of 'Teaching', since, the job markets were directly dependent on the degrees bestowed upon by the universities. However, the current situation has drastically shifted from this traditional scenario. Today the monopoly of universities to offer degrees as license for jobs is challenged by the plurality of recognized institutions in the society, which are need based and skill oriented. In the knowledge society of today, techno-aided learning has considerably changed the face of both learning and market requirements. Hence, the requirement of the position of an educational counselor is felt necessary in the Universities, where, 'knowledge learning' and 'market driven job' needs, will have to melt to match and create a web for those who would like to seek an opportunity to work or continue education. However, assisting with the details must also include the crucial task of helping students to address the psychosocial issues that they encounter. It is also important that teachers should be trained to recognize and identify students with mental illness and help them accordingly.

Stress Management Training for Youth

Any person engaged in a profession is subjected to varying amounts of stress due to professional activities, personal life and many a time due to combination of both. For success one has to learn to manage the stress so that it is not detrimental to personal or professional life. One has to develop a personality such that adversities and challenges are viewed as opportunities, which bring out the best in a person. Various approaches to stress management have been advocated but probably the best for Indian psyche and conditions is yoga. Practice of yoga has proved to be immensely helpful, in management.

This is an emerging area where all universities should give urgent attention. Today the youths are the most intolerant and frustrated group of our society. The young boys and girls are working and living under great pressures to cope up with the demands of the competitive world. It's important that they are trained in stress management skills so that they are capable to handle stress in various walks of their lives. Year after year our universities are producing thousands of degree and diploma holders. But the job market has very little hopes to share. Many more thousands are being added to the millions of frustrated jobless youth. It is high time for the university to take effective strategy to foresee danger and handle the crisis failing which; our country will have to feed a bunch of mentally unfit youth in the coming years. The youth while they are in universities should be trained to prepare themselves to face the crises in the job market and overcome it eventually.

Personal Growth and Satisfaction

Studying at a higher education level should offer student new challenges and goals. Whether these challenges involve independent living, juggling with family or a work commitment, or grasping new ideas and concepts, is obviously a very individual issue. For many students, the higher education experience has bought about a greater feeling of independence, self-discipline and growing confidence. Others have described the experience as one of personal growth and satisfaction. For most, it is about realizing one's full potential.

A typical college student has some, but not a lot, of free time. Most students want to use this time to relax and have fun. What they soon realize is that leisure activities can help develop intellectual and social skills that serve them well in careers and graduate programs. Students often report that their spare time activities have provided important experience and sharpened a number of skills, including: Leadership, Cultural understanding, Administration, Human relations, public speaking, writing, teaching, research, management, public relations, advertising, sales promotion, political communication, social service and public service.

Developing Skills and Subject Knowledge

Along with acquiring specialized subject knowledge, undergraduates should also be helped to develop and enhance other skills - perhaps this entails essay and report writing, study skills, time management skills, information gathering etc. Without a doubt, talent and above-average skills are what matters in today's knowledge-based economy. In a knowledge-based economy, only those with highest-skills advance and make progress in life. Thurow says:

> *"What is widening is not so much the wage gap between the averagely-skilled and the unskilled...but the gap between the averagely-skilled and the very skilled."*

Graduates follow a wide range of career paths and many may enter higher education with a clear view of the path they wish to follow. But for those who are unsure, or decide to change direction, the University should have a Career department to help the student to develop and plan his/her career, and to give practical advice. The department should provide a wide range of advice, services and information for students, which will give an insight into the different career options that are open to graduates.

Values and Ethics

For long term success and reputation in business, constant stress on practice of values and ethics is essential. Proper values and ethics are normally acquired by an individual in a society, which nurtures both. However, values and ethics are hard to acquire and practice in a society which is obsessed with success, pleasure, power, wealth etc. at any cost and by any method. In such a society it is faith, which leads a person to proper values and ethics. A study of values, ethics and faith, which incorporate carefully chosen exercises, requiring discretion is certainly helpful in acquiring and practicing these. Religious rituals and study of religious work are powerful motivations to acquiring values and ethics, if care is taken that religion does not degenerate into fundamentalism. Faith also sustains an individual in adversity.

Action Plan for Universities

The ordinances, syllabi and scheme of examination, at the

undergraduate level should be reformulated with a view to incorporate as many features of Education plus as possible and include courses corresponding to other features on a non-credit optional basis. Diploma and certificate courses on various aspects of Education Plus should be offered with the provision that these could be pursued, part time by undergraduate students (taking twice the time, corresponding to that for full time students). Participation by private agencies in the Education Plus programmes should be welcome.

Changing perspective of Higher Education

We have been consumed recently by internally derived changes in the structure and function of higher education. In particular the old concept of a university-essentially that of an ivory tower separate from society at large and therefore not contaminated by pressures of everyday life, is now virtually dead. University education is no longer funded publicly as an end in itself. Rather it is funded for more ulterior, even utilitarian purposes. In other words higher education is a means rather than an end. While universities remain dependent upon the public purse this is inevitable, but this also implies a degree of flexibility to change in relation to externally defined goals, which universities have felt it uncomfortable to come to terms with. It is the promotion of lifelong learning along with the complete growth of the student- it implies a set of qualitative and not just quantitative changes in the nature of teaching and learning.

Any and every University should:

- Set high-quality admission standards **and increase consideration of leadership and other dimensions of the whole student.**
- Nurture the individual student to insure highest probability of success. We must assume responsibility for the success of our students.
- Increase opportunities for all students to develop the academic and social connections that facilitate academic success and involvement in the life of the institution. Bring students and faculty into more frequent and productive interaction. **Double the number of small classes for undergraduates.**

- All students should have readily available opportunities for academic enrichment experiences appropriate to their educational goals. **Develop a systematic approach and infrastructure to facilitate opportunities for all students to have enrichment experiences, such as expanded honors courses, study-abroad experiences, interdisciplinary curricula, supplemental instruction, internships, cooperative education, and research opportunities. Where real world experiences are not possible simulated situations may help.**
- Continuously evaluate and adjust academic offerings and curricula to keep them relevant and strong.

Guidance and counseling has to be made an integral part of higher education to make it meaningful and purposeful for the students. A programme, if it is to make its impact felt on the growth and development of students and enhance the quantity and improve the quality of the educational programme as a whole, there needs to be set up a well organized structure covering the three major functions of the programme viz, *adjustmental, orientational* and *developmental.* It is desirable that the upcoming universities and institutes build this provision into their organizational structure at the planning stage itself and the old universities suitably add this provision into their educational programme so that the students may avail of this service easily and profitably.

Personality Development Cell

There is an urgent need today to establish a *Personality Development Cell* in every university to deal exclusively with the psychological and personal issues of the students and to train them in numerous skills viz. communication skills, public speaking skills, developing confidence, increased memory and concentration power, problem solving ability, goal setting and time management skills. Universities must plan out some practical training programmes to develop new enthusiasm in youth for work, responsibility and living. Such programmes will help them overcome fear and timidity and will enhance their ability to express ideas and feelings effectively.

Education today is an enterprise of universal dimensions, huge and far reaching, and the aims have universal application. Education for individual excellence and for nation- building is missed in many of the colleges, which under a mistaken definition of secularism do not even offer a prayer at the beginning of the day's work. Courses in value education need to be conducted for students, teachers and administrators, so as to ensure a value-imbibing atmosphere in the whole campus. As Swami Vivekananda has said, institutions of higher education are meant for man-making and character-building and unless such a mission is undertaken in all seriousness by higher educational institutions, the nation and the world would continue to be destroyed by violence and other evils. [S.Laxmi][10]

Beyond their traditional academic role the Universities should aspire to achieve the goal of value education by the following: sensitizing about values to the prospective teachers and varied workforce produced by the universities, reforms in school curricula for value education, development of knowledge and research base for value education, collaborations and liaison with other national and international institutions and academia engaged in work in this field.

Campus placement cell

Institutes and colleges of professional courses e.g. MBA, B.Tech, MBBS, and Law etc offer job placement facilities for their final year students. They have an independent campus placement cell headed by a professor. Universities should also cater to the job requirements of their pass outs and should run such placement cells with a clearly specified vision and programme. Such cells should keep on studying the current trends and requirements in the occupational world and try to prepare the universities pass outs for the jobs they are suited for. The Cell should also provide occupational information, training for the interview, conduct of mock interviews and training for effective presentation.

Counseling Cell

Even though the area of academic advising is limited to academics, it is important for advisers to attend to psychosocial issues that may affect students' academic performance and to educate students about these issues. Once students are informed, they have a better understanding of how to improve their academic performance, especially if it means benefiting from personal counseling at the college's counseling center. They are then better able to make informed choices. Every University and a large college should have a counseling center headed by a trained professional counseling officer who should be a Ph.D or possess Master's Degree in Psychology and Counseling, with considerable counseling experience. The Center should be situated at a convenient place so as to facilitate the provisions of counseling services for the whole university community and the colleges in the immediate vicinity. The faculty members can refer students to it and students too would like to visit it to get help in their problems and anxieties. The center should discharge the following functions:

- Give assistance to individuals and small groups of students and staff members with special educational, vocational and personal problems
- Every teachers should be trained to identify students with problems both mental and emotional
- Give assistance to the university in developing, advising and counseling programmes and consultation on special psychological problems
- Provide psychological testing facilities for the university both for individuals and groups
- It would be ideal if the Counseling Center includes special clinics and laboratories for speech and hearing problems, study skills and reading improvement.

The Organizational set-up

A **Guidance and Counseling Committee** under the Chairmanship of the Vice Chancellor should be statutorily established in the University to look after the youths' higher education beyond academics. The Personality Development Cell, Placement Cell and Counseling Cell of the University should function under this Guidance and Counseling Committee in which at least one representative of each of the following should represent as a member: The University Employment Information and Guidance Bureau (UEIGB), Dean of Students, Heads of Departments of Psychology, Education and Management, in charges of Personality Development Cell, Campus Placement Cell, and Counseling Cell, Academic Advisor of Student Advisory Bureau (SAB). If the number of students exceeds 1000, assistant counseling officers may be appointed. One assistant counseling officer may be ideally for every 100 students.

An effective guidance and counseling programme staffed with adequate qualified personnel and equipped with adequate tools does cost much money. Studies do suggest that potentially an effective programme of guidance can make significant contribution to student development. The real question, therefore, may not be "can the college or university or even the state afford guidance"? But rather, "can the college or university or state afford not to have guidance?" It should be apparent that it is not the question whether the facility of guidance and counseling for college and university student should be provided or not, but only a question of how soon and how good!

Extension: the Third dimension of Higher Education

Universities and Institutes of higher learning are large repositories of knowledge, manpower and physical resources. They cannot function and exist in isolation of the society and communities where they are located. They have an obligation to cater to the overall and diverse learning needs of the segments of the neighboring people and communities. If the University system has to discharge its social obligations and duties adequately it must embrace extension as the third important dimension and give it the same status as teaching and research. Extension is a new and extremely significant area. It caters to the community and overall and diverse learning needs of all the segments of the people of the community while generating new knowledge simultaneously. Once new body of knowledge is generated or innovations made, there usually exists a 'gap' between the existing knowledge of the client and the new knowledge available.

Extension 'bridges' the gap in knowledge bringing desirable planned change in the behavior complex of the people with a view to help them live better by learning new /or improving existing vocations and enterprises. The Kothari Commission, the India Education Commission in 1964 comprehensively examined and reviewed the entire educational system and emphasized 'Extension as the third dimension of higher education'. It introduced the trinity of Teaching, Research & Extension in higher education. This was necessitated by the fact that the education has to be made relevant to real life situations, so that the learners cannot be alienated from the society, and they develop a sense of responsibility towards society.

Extension education takes different forms viz. community development strategies, co-operative education, agricultural extension services, extra-mural activities and the like, which link experts with the target population through a given medium. Agricultural extension has been at the forefront, since the predominant occupation of the rural population is agriculture. All development-oriented institutions have in a sense the mission to "extend" their message. Certain units are, however, expressly charged with that function. Extension education was pioneered in Africa by the British colonial authorities, and it was accepted in Nigeria in the early 1970s that a university had to use its total intellectual capability in the service of the nation. While a university should foster the expansion of the frontiers of knowledge, it should utilize such knowledge to respond to the needs of society.

Extension education is a major contribution, since a measure of the effective implementation of a university's role is widespread involvement and participation. To be effective, however, an extension department has to possess societal "feelers", and to have the expertise to diagnose the emergent needs, demands, aspirations and expectations of people living in complex communities. This means that if the activities of extra-mural, continuing education and community service departments of universities are to be appropriate, they must adopt a non-formal approach. The "opening up" process of extension work is certainly not top-down nor even a two-way communication between top and bottom, but is a dialogue between equals.[11]

Retired people are not tired these days. The services of these people, who are experts in their fields, can be taken to provide skill and knowledge to youth and adults in diverse areas. Example the music faculty of any university can start evening classes for those who want to learn music, these learners may be from the university itself or outside the campus. Similarly the Yoga and the astrology department can start small courses in their field and the elderly population of the society can be provided a social platform to keep them engaged and offer their expertise.

Employability is an important aspect of Education Plus and is a full chapter in this book.

Specific References

1. Deborah Meier, (1995) *The Power of Their Ideas: Lessons for America from a Small School in Harlem.* Beacon Press, Boston.
2. Peterson, G. W. (1986). Generic problem solving skills: Are they misnomers as constructs of educational outcomes? (ERIC Document Reproduction Service No. ED 271 516)
3. Sodha, M.S. (2000), *Education Plus*, University News, 38(20), 1-4.
4. https://www.msde.gov.in/pmkvy.html
5. UNESCO, (1996), '*Learning: The Treasure Within,*' Report of the International Commission on Education for the Twenty-first Century (Delors Report), UNESCO, Paris.
6. UNESCO, (1998), Higher Education in the Twenty-first Century: Vision and Action, UNESCO, Paris.
7. Klein, D.B. *Mental Hygiene*
8. UGC Xth Plan Guidelines. New Delhi: University Grants Commission, 2004.
9. *Dissertation Abstracts International*. Section A (ISSN: 0419-4209) Michigan. USA: Pro Quest Information and Learning.
10. S. Laxmi, *Revamping Higher Education*, in *Indian University System: Revitalization and Reform*, by M.V. Mathur, Ramesh K Arora and Meena Sogani. Wiley Eastern Limited, New Delhi. Pp. 167-168.
11. https://www.researchgate.net/publication/311370766_EXTENSION_THE_THIRD_DIMENSION_OF_HIGHER_EDUCATION [accessed Sep 03 2018].

General References

Advisory Committee to Study Graduate Education in the CSU. 1989. *Graduate education in the California State University: Meeting public needs consistent with educational priorities.* Office of the Chancellor: Long Beach, CA.

Bates, S. D. (2003, August 1). Don't forget the details: A call for balance in academic advising. *The Mentor: An Academic Advising Journal,* 6(1).

Corey, G., & Corey, M. S. (2002). *I never knew I had a choice: Explorations in personal growth*. Pacific Grove, CA: Brooks/Cole.

Council of Graduate Schools. 1990. *A policy statement: Organization and administration of graduate education.* Council of Graduate Schools: Washington, D.C.

Ellemers, N., Spears, R., & Doosje, B. (2002). Self and social identity. *Annual Review of Psychology: Self and Social Identity*.

Education and National Development. Report of the Education Commission 1964-66. NCERT 1971. Pp 497.

Frank, K. S. (2000). Ethical consideration and obligations. In V. Gordon & W. Habley (Eds.), *Academic Advising: A Comprehensive Handbook* (pp. 44–57). San Francisco: Jossey- Bass. Guanipa-Ho, C., & Guanipa, J. A. Ethnic identity and adolescence.

Johnson, D., and Rudolph, A. (2001). *Critical Issue: Beyond Social Promotion and Retention—Five Strategies to Help Students Succeed.* Naperville, IL: Learning Point Associates, www.learningpt.org.

San Francisco State University. 1991. Self-study report: Prepared for the Accrediting Commission for Senior Colleges and Universities, Western Association of Schools and Colleges. San Francisco State University: San Francisco, CA.

Top ten issues identified by students. Retrieved September 27, 2003, from Wichita State University, Letters and Sciences Academic Adviser's Handbook *The Chronicle of Higher Education,* July 7, 1995.

Reflection - 6

Academia - Industry Interaction: Need of the Hour

Introduction

Academia-industry interaction, a long felt need and often discussed subject has become all the more relevant and visible in the past few years, primarily because the complementary nature and mutual benefits of such an interaction have come to be appreciated by both sides. Universities and industry, which for long have been operating in separate domains, are converging to create synergies. This is primarily due to the need for innovation, creativity and continuous up-gradation of skills, required by the industry for keeping pace with technological development and competition. The constantly changing management paradigms, in response to growing complexity of the business environment today have also necessitated these two to come closer. Higher educational institutions not only contribute skilled human resource to business and industry, but it also contributes in various intangible ways. The intersecting needs and mutually interdependent relationship requires identifying means of strengthening academia-industry partnership.[1]

Higher education and research are essential components of culture, socio-economic, and environmentally sustainable development of individuals, community and nations. Since providing education relevant to the changing society is essential, existing institutions are required to start new courses. The UGC is encouraging colleges and universities to generate their own resources to run relevant courses in conformity with the present and future needs. TQM consists of long term planning, capacity building, human resource development and bench marking as inevitable ingredients of quality striving institutions. Privatization of higher education is being advocated in view of changing economic policy of liberalization and globalization. There is a consensus in favour of upward revision of fee structure and creation of funds from sources other than government agencies.

Industry is an organization, considered as prime user or employer of the university products, namely knowledge and graduates. There is a strong relationship between what should be supplied by the university and what is required in the market, field and industry. Various schemes have been initiated which aim at promoting university-industry interaction towards problem-solving and sharing of intellectual, equipment and resources of each other. Benefits of academic-industry interaction have been visualized as panacea for resolving extreme resource crunch in universities and provision of intellect to the industries for their modernization.

Academia and industry are two sides of the same coin- the economy. Some may argue that academia exists only for knowledge creation and dissemination, which has no connection with wealth and that industry, exists only for wealth, and has no connection with knowledge. The fact is that to afford pursuit of knowledge, there has to be some one in the background working on the practical aspects of wealth creation. While the industries need specialized skills and analytical approach to either solve problems on hand or to innovate, which may not be readily available within its own knowledge base; the academia is in a position to provide such support to industries with an affordable and significant compensation in terms of consultancy or investments by industry in creating or expanding infrastructure of academic institutions. Further, as the technology is increasingly becoming a strong weapon of competitiveness at national and international level, it is important that India moves to a higher level of technology competence. Therefore, industry-academia interaction has to grow to a level, which ensures technological advances in all fields and drives the country on the road of economic growth and independence.

Collaboration between universities and industries is critical for skills development (education and training), the generation, acquisition, and adoption of knowledge (innovation and technology transfer), and the promotion of entrepreneurship (start-ups and spin-offs). The benefits of university-industry linkages are wide-reaching; they can help coordinate R&D agendas and avoid duplications, stimulate additional private R&D investment (additionally effect), and exploit synergies and complementarities of scientific and technological capabilities. University-industry collaboration can also expand the relevance of research carried out in public institutions, foster the commercialization of public R&D outcomes, and increase the mobility of labor between public and private sectors. The benefits of university-industry collaboration are also evident in developing countries. For example, a study in Chile and Colombia shows that collaboration with universities substantially increased the propensity of firms to introduce new products and to patent [Marotta, Blom, and Thorn 2007].[2]

Firms and universities are increasingly finding it mutually beneficial to collaborate. On one hand, private firms are progressively adopting open innovation strategies to better access and integrate external sources of knowledge, leading to a stronger interest in collaboration with universities. On the other hand, since the 1990s, the strategic mission of universities has moved beyond the tradition of teaching and research toward a "third mission" related to better addressing the needs of industry and contributing directly to economic growth and development. The three university missions have given rise to the distinct concepts of teaching university, Research University and entrepreneurial university. University-industry collaboration may take place under all of these university regimes, although it will have a distinct focus on training in the teaching university, on R&D in the research university, and on technology commercialization in entrepreneurial university.

Need for Academia-Industry Interface

With changing international economic order, globalization of education, need for quality assurance in higher education and provision of need-based educational opportunities, and constant changes in the market forces, higher education needs to be constantly reoriented and made flexible and diversified so as to keep pace with these developments and if possible show leadership in some of the areas of its concern. The orientation of traditional basic research conducted in institutions of higher learning is gradually undergoing changes so as to link it with the immediate socio-economic needs of the country, and higher education curricula are being constantly revised so as to meet the requirements of the contemporary society. A major concern of higher education planners and academicians, the world over, has been to link universities and other research institutions with industries and other market forces.

Academia- Industry interface could be defined as interactive and collaborative arrangement between academic institutions and business corporations for the achievement of mutually inclusive goals and objectives. Traditionally, business schools look for placements and internships for their students and the industry for fresh recruits who are well trained and equipped with the right ***KSA*** (knowledge, skills and attitude) and empowered to contribute to the organization's growth. [Bisoux, 2003][3] has explored the relationship between the academia and the industry. He states that corporations are placing growing emphasis on finding the "right person". This forces the business schools to think more carefully about the right person for the industry, and therefore the role of industry in the entire business school model becomes important.

The future of our country is going to be shaped in our classrooms since the survival of the domestic industry will depend on its technology leadership. India has emerged as one of the largest economies of the world and will continue its rapid urbanization and economic development with the aspiration of achieving double-digit growth in the coming years. Sustenance of this momentum largely depends upon our ability to leverage the vast pool of untapped human resource in our academic institutions for enhancing competitiveness in the global market place.

Today, there exists a huge gap between the rapidly evolving skill needs of Indian business/industry and those provided by our higher educational system. There is a growing realization amongst the government, academic institutions and the industry, of the urgent need to bridge the skill gap. There is a need to adopt a holistic approach to the new age academia-industry interaction, which should address issues like improvement in governance of academic institutions and industry linkages, building centers of excellence, effective industry involvement in education related policy issues etc. Similarly, the academic fraternity needs to come out with their creative thoughts and share these with industry for their actualization. The government has made a massive increase in budgetary allocations for education and R&D sectors, besides providing tax exemptions in R&D expenditures. It has also acknowledged the importance of public-private partnership for meeting long term goals of the country.

India has the potential of becoming a global hub for providing high-end manufacturing services to the world. There is still a need to have a clear and unambiguous perception in the direction of leveraging strength towards actualization of excellence. The government should draw upon a wide variety of policy initiatives to help create synergies between efficiency, objectives and energy of Indian industries with creativity, knowledge and competence of Indian academia to exploit emerging opportunities. A corollary to this thought is that India should strive to become a global hub for excellent education and research, in conformance with the needs of the industry.

The close partnership between industries and universities is fundamental for the social and economic development. These are eight advantages of this interaction:

1. Strengthening of the entrepreneurship

Entrepreneurship must be stimulated in the academic environment. In the United States, there are many business schools that are reference to the world, such as Harvard and Wharton, whose professors continue working in companies. In Brazil, the focus is more on administration than on business, and, frequently, the professors are not stimulated to conciliate the academic life with the daily routine in industries.

2. Transformation of companies into educational environments

The universities are educational environments, while companies are seen as training places. However, the interaction with the academic world may stimulate industries to become educational environments, with a pedagogic project and development of abilities and competences.

3. Transfer of knowledge and generation of value

As natural environments where knowledge is stimulated and valued, the universities may transmit this value to the business environment. From this point on, they also learn how to get resources by negotiating inventions to become innovative. An example of this is Google, which was created in the university environment and has become a very profitable business.

4. Interaction among different cultures

The entrepreneurial environment, as well as the academic one, has their own set of beliefs and values. By interacting, industries and universities may harmonize their cultures and improve them by incorporating what is of best in each one of them.

5. Professionals that meet the social and economic demands

The university must be concerned to produce professionals with competences to meet the social demands. Besides, the students must leave the university with abilities to negotiate and acknowledge the economic value of their competences. More than workers, the universities should be poles to form entrepreneurs.

6. Incorporation of the market vision by the universities

It is necessary to acknowledge that the inventions as well as the formation of professionals have a social and economic value. Students graduating from the public schools need to offer a compensation for the education financed by society. Students who drop out of school should pay for the years invested in their education.

7. Stimulation to innovation

In the innovating environment, universities focus in creating novelties and companies in producing the new products in series and cheaper for the consumer. Besides, the universities may stimulate startups. Large companies, in general, improve products, while new industries are innovating and come to challenge the large businesses.

8. Growth of competitiveness

There are at the universities a multiplying effect and the generation of an innovation cycle: academic curricula with more innovating contents and the formation of professionals who generate innovating products and are more entrepreneurial. More successful products and companies generate more jobs, taxes, wealth that create better environments and demand for universities and innovating companies.[4]

Academia-Industry Interaction the World Over

Developed economies the world over have recognized the symbiotic relationship between academia and industry and have emerged as a role model for the interaction process. In the U.S., the U.K. and other European countries, there is healthy intermingling of the faculty, students and research scholars from the academia with the managers and engineers in the industry. The US university system has been extremely practical from the very beginning; it has been highly focused on utilitarian pursuits like increasing efficiency in agriculture or ways and means of progress in other domains for betterment of economy; basic research is not the only priority.

The fact that most top universities in the US, such as Harvard, Massachusetts Institutes of Technology, Yale or Carnegie Melon are private universities, set up by industrialists who had a vision and who could foresee the advantage of investing in the educational system, shows that if it wants, the industry can take the initiative and significantly contribute to knowledge creation. All these universities are heavily interlinked with industry and have given rise to powerhouses like the Silicon Valley. In comparison, there are fewer private universities in the UK with the prominent ones being the University of Buckingham and the Richmond University. Germany has 83 private universities and Japan has nearly 600 of these. A country like Switzerland also has an advanced private system of higher education. It ensures a high degree of academia- industry interaction and collaboration for both curriculum as well as research.[5]

In India, over the years the industry and academia have been seen as the North Pole and the South Pole rather than as two sides of the same coin. Notwithstanding the recommendations of the various education commissions set up after Independence and the emphasis in the National Education Policy, industry-academia interaction still remains marginal and largely confined to a few top institutions such as the IITs, the IIMs and a few CSIR laboratories. The exception of course, is agriculture, where there is a long and continuing tradition of agro industries, based on the outcome of the research by agricultural universities. However, this broad sectoral involvement is qualitatively normally different from the individualized and customized partnership that industry-academia interaction is, though customization is also entering agriculture through biotechnology. There have been excellent examples of academia-industry collaboration in India in the pre-independence era in which the Tatas set up the Indian Institute of Science in Bangalore, the Xavier's Lab and a Management Institution in Jamshedpur or the Birlas set an institution of technology in Pilani. All these are centers of excellence in their own right today. All these institutes were set up with altruistic motive other than immediate profit.

If we look at the academia, the curricula in most institutes are outdated and there is shortage of faculty because a career in industry is far more lucrative than one in an institute. There is not enough marketable research, and the quality of education has declined to an extent that there are not enough employable graduates who can be productive.

Industry-academia interaction does not mean exclusion of other interactions viz. amongst academia itself and also between students and teachers. Multidimensional interactions must include all the stakeholders to ensure that everybody is on the same frequency. Just as not enough has happened in industry-academia interactions, there is a lot to be desired on intra- academic interactions also. The great centers of excellence IIT's and IIM's can do wonders as a single brand if they all come together on a single platform. Other institutions can also play a supporting role in such a network.

Industry-Academia Interaction

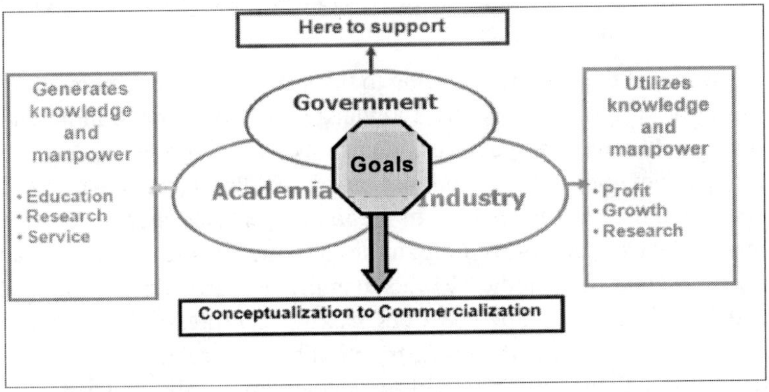

The above figure is a representation of the industry-academia interaction.

Teaching, research and extension are known as the trinity of higher education. Teaching is the basic activity of communicating knowledge to students and stimulating their interest. Research not only extends the frontiers of knowledge but lends depth, breadth and a certain authority and authenticity to teaching. Extension exploits existing knowledge for economically and socially beneficial purposes and puts the validity of this knowledge to test in real world conditions, raising new questions for research, which again feed back into teaching and extension; so the cycle continues.

Of the three major systems in academia — government laboratories, IITs / IIMs and universities — the first two are distinctly stronger in terms of management, resources, expertise and reputation. They should, therefore, provide the major thrust by co-opting reputed university departments as partners in all major research and consultancy projects. As teaching is a major responsibility of universities, research and consultancy should not be at the expense of teaching but only as a value-adding activity. Teachers, junior or senior, should engage in both teaching and research/consultancy as synergizing modules. Universities are, or at least ought to be, the prime repositories of up-to-date and advanced levels of knowledge in different fields. Especially in knowledge society, industry and business are the main users and beneficiaries of such knowledge. One would, therefore, think it natural, almost inevitable, for universities and industry to come together in a close, constructive collaboration to use such knowledge for mutual benefit and that of society.

Some of the benefits accruing to the industry with this interaction would be using the academic knowledge base to improve industrial cost, quality and competitive dimensions, reducing dependence on foreign know-how and expenditure on internal R&D and updating and upgrading the knowledge base of the industry's professionals through professional development programmes designed by the academia. The faculty's exposure to industry leads to improved curricula and widened and deepened teaching perspectives resulting in professional graduates of a high caliber to man the industry. Similarly, the academia would be benefited with the satisfaction of seeing their knowledge and expertise being used for socially useful and productive purposes, widening and deepening of the curricula and the perspectives of teachers and researchers and earning additional resources for a system severely constrained in this regard. Securing training and final placements for students are much easier on account of the recognition earned from and the relationships established with industry.

The accreditation process for technical institutions (offering engineering, management and computer courses) should specifically highlight the potential and capabilities for training, problem-oriented research and consultancy and give a separate star rating in this aspect in addition to the overall institutional rating now being given. This should also be given for social sciences disciplines such as economics, commerce, psychology and sociology.

Before drafting a new Five-Year Plan, the Planning Commission usually farms out research projects on specialized sectoral studies to university departments. This practice deserves to be continued and expanded further. Apart from motivating the academics, this would enable industry to readily identify competent departments for giving assignments with confidence. Though the public sector is shrinking, major PSUs should, as a matter of policy, utilize available expertise from academia, wherever feasible.

In addition to the accreditation rating mentioned above, the UGC, the AICTE and the CSIR could prepare a list of departments and their area of specialization and consultancy competence and operate an industry-academia interaction exchange in every State (on the lines of an employment exchange) which any academic institution or industry can access. While sanctioning departments of excellence in universities, the University Grants Commission should keep in view the relevance of these to the needs and problems of industry. Not withstanding existing cells every major academic institution should have a suitably structured academia-industry interaction council headed by the head of the institution, which should promote and remove bottlenecks in the interaction. At the annual conferences of trade and industry, associations such as FICCI and CII, academics should make presentations on academia's problem-solving, research and consultancy capabilities.

Since the industry in general does not have a high opinion of academia's usefulness to them, it is for the latter to take the initiative to break the ice. Some of these initiatives would be:

- Including pro-active and positive-minded professionals from industry and business in syndicates and boards of study,
- Using practicing professionals from industry as part-time guest faculty,
- Securing training/project attachments for senior students and research scholars in industry,
- Exploiting contacts with alumni who are successful in industry and business,
- Offering capacity building courses for professionals in industry, as this is a safe, inexpensive trial interaction for the latter,
- Offering inexpensive consultancy to small and medium industries, which cannot afford expensive consultants.

Beard, 1994[6] has a number of recommendations towards increasing and enhancing academia-industry interface, which include:

- Greater degree of industry-institution collaboration to integrate employer's needs into the programmes on offer;

- Real involvement with industry to allow students to gain valuable practical experience and also to facilitate development of business;
- Improve the programmes by encouraging the participation of a number of guest speakers who can offer their own practical experiences;
- Academic staff should be encouraged to keep their skills updated by undertaking practical consultancy on regular basis.

The recent successes of Indian entrepreneurs in IT and process and product outsourcing have generated a new self-confidence in Indian industry to take on global competition, unlike in the past when there was near-total dependence on foreign collaboration for achieving any breakthrough. Groups such as the TVS, Bajaj and Tata have successfully developed models in-house, without any foreign collaboration. The garments industry, even in small towns like Karur and Tirupur, is looking forward confidently to facing global competition after the removal of quotas from January 2005. Indian companies have won prestigious international awards such as the Deming prize. Wipro and Infosys recently signed MoUs with some universities for collaboration. The atmosphere, therefore, is ripe for academia to exploit to its advantage this new ambience of confidence and self-reliance in industry.

Sincere efforts have been made on both sides to overcome the lack of communication and non-converging objectives and ambitions. Today there is a healthy cooperation with academia supporting industry sponsored projects at the industries or at exclusive research parks or enrolling industry personnel for part time/full time higher education programs. Similarly, industries too approach academia for widening its knowledge base, enhancing the product value with various studies, performance evaluation, qualifying through standard test procedures, reverse engineering, re-engineering etc. While the short-term objectives of the industry could still be to stay ahead in competition or increasing profit margin there is an increasing appreciation of the long-term benefits of such associations. There are numerous examples of industry, sponsoring research with mutually agreed terms and conditions, processed through exclusive desks created at academic institutions for ease of completing procedural formalities quickly and directly engaging the actual research work.

There are however, some inhibiting factors working both from the industry's side and academia's side, which limit a healthy interaction. Industry's insensitivity to, and/or lack of awareness of the resource potential of the academia, a blind herd-like obsession with expensive, high-profile professional consultants, easy availability of foreign know-how, compulsions of existing technical collaboration agreements, bad experience of earlier interactions with academia and anxiety to keep problems and breakthroughs confidential for fear of losing the competitive edge, may inhibit the industry from believing in and interacting with the academic fraternity. Similarly, apathy towards applied research and extension, reluctance to leave the comfort zone of pure teaching; inadequate marketing of its strengths to industry, lack of a critical mass of experts and specialized technical infrastructure, overspecialized loyalties, reluctance to collaborate in inter-disciplinary problem-solving, unhelpful, restrictive internal policies and procedures, previous frustrating academicians' attempts to collaborate with industry are certain inhibiting factors working on the academia's side.

There are still many issues, which need attention, debate and discussion towards evolving at a viable model for the benefit of both the academia and industries. Issues like Intellectual Property Rights, adhering to time schedule, objective oriented approach to problem solving, efficient management of resources and monitoring at regular intervals are the areas, where differences in opinion or approach may occur. The model evolves with experience, structured analysis of the interfacing problems and seeking the solution through joint efforts. This has already been achieved by the mature institutions and industries and needs to be followed by others in the right spirit. A good example in this respect has been set up by BHEL. It has had a long association with various academic institutions in collaborative development activities through its corporate R&D Division at Hyderabad or directly at the manufacturing divisions level interacting with various IIT's, NITs and colleges specialized in certain subject areas. It had also been interacting with universities abroad for specific consultancy services from time to time.

University-Research Parks: Enhancing Academia-Industry Interaction

National governments can further shape university-industry links by developing science parks in the vicinity of universities and by spurring university research spin-offs and start-ups with university connections, for example through public venture capital and grants to entrepreneurs. A university research park is a "cluster of technology-based organizations that are located on or near a university campus in order to benefit from the university's knowledge base and ongoing research. The university not only transfers knowledge but expects to develop knowledge more effectively from the association with the tenants in the research park." The Association of University Research Parks (AURP)[7] refers to university research parks as property based ventures that promote a university's research and development activities as well as local economic development. Effective parks can aid in the transfer of technology and business skills between university and industry teams, encourage the creation of start-ups, and promote technology-led economic development for the community, region and the country.

Science parks are intended to create clusters and promote collaboration between firms and research institutions, and they often include business incubators to support spin-off and start-up companies. The number of science park initiatives has exploded in both developed and developing countries, although examples of failure abound where ambitious science parks turned into no more than real estate players with unsustainable financials. In particular, there is a lack of compelling evidence of success of these initiatives in low and middle income countries. [Yusuf, 2007][8] points out numerous examples of such failed attempts in China. Despite the potential benefits of science parks and university spin-offs, not all regions and countries have the necessary endowments to achieve success in developing science and technology parks. Governments that aim to create these research clusters are advised to be cautious and to design the park in accordance with a realistic assessment of the expected results in a given context.

While parks gain knowledge and prestige from their university partners, the universities gain as well. Association with a successful park can bring multiple benefits to a university such as: higher publication rates, more successful patenting activities, greater ability to hire eminent scientists in the long run and an ability to garner larger extramural grants. A result of successful institute-industry partnership in the context of a research park is a shift in the institute curricula towards more applied research that is also reflected by improved student placements.

A university research park provides an "essential tool for institutions with an entrepreneurial and innovative culture that hope to benefit from complicated partnerships on a global scale." It can provide the physical space and facilities not generally available on a university campus; it can do proprietary or classified research, which is not easily done in an academic environment; it can provide a platform to a large off-campus work force to achieve the clustering, resonance and mutual energy of people working and thinking together and finally, it can uniquely bring in the many non-university interests required by complex partnerships, including private industry services, security for confidential business activities and government facilities.

Research parks are increasingly seen as a means to create dynamic clusters that accelerate economic growth and international competitiveness, encouraging greater collaboration among universities, research laboratories, and large and small companies, providing a means to help convert new ideas into the innovative technologies for the market. In this way, research parks are recognized to be a "proven tool to create successful new companies, sustain them, attract new ones-especially in the S&T and innovative sector and make existing companies more successful through the use of R& D." Research parks are no longer a developed world phenomenon. Parks can be found in more than 60 countries at all stages of development. Most research parks are planned as part of a national strategy for industrial competitiveness. Technological development at many research parks is increasingly integrated with university research, with faculty working with private firms and firms renting laboratories and incubator space in universities.

China and Singapore are among those undertaking substantial national efforts to develop research parks on significant scale, which have scientific and innovative potential. These efforts have the potential to shift the terms of global competition especially in leading technological sectors.

Situation in India

Before 1990 there was little or no encouragement for the government-industry academic partnerships that characterize modern Science and Technology parks. As a result no formal research parks were located near universities, although some inter-sector partnerships were created informally within campuses. By about 1999, S&T park movement began to take off as India's entrepreneurial spirit was being liberated. Indian research parks are not generally associated with universities. The bigger ones have varying mix of tenants and partnerships. Some of the examples are 140 acre, 400 crore Shapoorji Pallonji Biotech Park near Hyderabad; 218 acre Marine Biotech Park near Visakhapatnam; 250 crore Maharashtra Biotech Park near Pune; the Uttar Pradesh Biotech Park set up in collaboration with the CSIR, universities and industries in Lucknow; the 20 acre Golden Jubilee Biotech Park for Women (2001), the first Asian biotech park dedicated exclusively to furthering the careers of women entrepreneurs.

University based Research Parks motivate innovation through the 'idea-factory' approach by bringing three kinds of minds and experience together viz. that of the faculty, who have the knowledge of fundamentals; students, enthused with ideas and the spirit to conquer the world and S&T personnel from the industry, with their ability to convert the ideas into marketable products. Some university-initiated societies exist within the educational institutions with similar goals as the research parks. These include the Society for Innovation and Development in IISc, Bangalore, started in 1991, the Society for Innovation and Entrepreneurship, started in 2004 on the campus of IIT-Bombay with support from the Department of S&T and the Innovation and Incubation Center, started by IIT-Kanpur in partnership with the Small Industries Development Bank of India (SIDBI). The Industrial Consultancy and Sponsored Research Center in IIT Madras started in 1973 and expanded in scope in the 90's.[9]

Case study of IIT-Madras Research Park

IIT-Madras Research Park (IITMRP) put up by IIT Madras with the formal permission of the Government, is the first attempt of its kind to create a full-fledged University based Research Park in India. It is an independent company promoted by IIT-Madras with support of the State Government, MHRD and IITM alumni. By design it is located outside the campus but within walking distance. It is planned to have an area of 1.5 million square feet, built in three phases, to house R&D activities of companies who wish to work with IIT-Madras as well as companies to be incubated.

There are important synergies to be gained by leveraging university expertise and knowledge, and by offering higher education opportunities for the park's employees. The goal is to have some 5000 development engineers and finishing schools for up to 5000 students per year. Some 5% of R&D personnel are expected to teach as adjunct faculty, while 10% are expected to register for part-time masters and Ph.D. programs at IIT-Madras.

To the extent that this and other parks can attract highly qualified individuals to R&D, India could become a 'design house' that develops higher quality products, participate in international standards bodies, and develop intellectual property rights. To advance such goals IITMRP will feature infrastructure for start-ups, availability of venture capital, and consultancy and prototype firms in the vicinity. Some 15% of park space will be reserved for start-ups and for training companies at concessional or deferred rental. The remaining 85% of the space will be rented or leased on a long term to companies leveraging R&D partnerships with the university.

India needs at least 25 URPs to promote innovation and entrepreneurship. Twelve S&T institutes of national importance form the backbone of Indian Higher Education. These include the seven IITs, five of which were formed soon after independence in 1950's; one was added in 1995 and another in 2001. Eight more IITs and five IISERs have been added since 2006. The strong national recognition and status of the IITs makes them logical anchors for research parks as they provide leadership in Science and Engineering. To begin with one such park associated with and set up in the vicinity of each of the twelve S&T institutes of national importance is needed. In the second phase, other IITs and IISERs should be enabled to set up Research Parks to promote innovation and competitiveness.

The IITM Research Park has been created by nearly a decade of hard work despite the generally cooperative attitude of both the Government of Tamil Nadu and the Ministry of Human Resource Development.

Vision for Future

The concerns over academia-industry interaction have been widely discussed by all concerned many a times. The need of the hour is urgent action to make up for the lost time. The public funded R&D (Protection, Utilization and Regulation of Intellectual Property) Bill 2007 is one such step, which can go a long way in better utilization of government-funded research work. Other steps required in increasing academia-industry collaborations are greater alignment of curricula with the requirements of industry and more practical training sessions for students in all streams. So far it has only been students on the technical side who have been taking up internships in industry. While basic research will continue to require government support, applied R&D will have to be supported more actively by the industry.

To conclude, an all round excellence of higher education institutes and supporting linkages is essential for the health and progress of science and its utilization. It is only when faculty, students, research and curricula are all aligned with industry that a healthy interaction and the synergy between academia and industry can take place.

Specific References

1. http://www.iosrjournals.org/iosr-jrme/papers/Vol-5%20Issue-6/Version-2/C05621214.pdf
2. Marotta, D., M. Mark, A. Blom, and K. Thorn. 2007. "Human Capital and University-Industry Linkages' Role in Fostering Firm Innovation: An Empirical Study of Chile and Colombia." Policy Research Working Paper 4443, World Bank, Washington, DC.
3. Bisoux Tricia, *"New Directions in Global Education*", Bized January/February 2003 AACSB Publication, pp. 34-37.

4. http://www.senaipr.org.br/conferenciainternacional/us/8-benefits-of-the-interaction-between-universities-and-industry-2-31194-313693.shtml
5. https://www.ncbi.nlm.nih.gov/pmc/articles/PMC3369181/
6. Beard C., "Educating the star fleet captain-making business schools more relevant to their stakeholders, *Working paper*, University of Paisley, June 1994.
7. AURP Website accessed at http://www.au1p.net/about/whatis.cfm, July 11, 2008.
8. Yusuf, S. 2007. "University-Industry Links: Policy Dimensions." In How Universities Promote Economic Growth, edited by S. Yusuf and K. Nabeshima, 1–26. Washington DC.: World Bank.
9. Ananth, M. S., (2011). 'University Research Parks', *Frontiers in Science and Technology: Abstracts of Plenary Sessions,* at the 98th Indian Science Congress, January 3-7.

General References

1. Altbach Philip G., "*Higher education and WTO: Globalisation Among*", International Higher Education, No.3, The Boston College Centre for International Higher Education.
2. Albert N. Link and John T. Scott, (2006). "U.S. University Research Parks," *Journal of Productivity Analysis* 25(1): 43-55.
3. C.D. Monte, Jr. President, University of Maryland, (2001). *Keynote Address II*, Report of Symposium "Understanding Research, Science and Technology Parks: Global Best Practices", p. 49, National Academies Press, Washington, DC.
4. G. Wayne Clough, (2007). "The Role of the Research University in Fostering Innovation", The Americas Competitiveness Forum, June 12.
5. Panda, S.K., (1995). 'University-Industry Interaction in International Perspective', *Liaison Cells for University-Industry Interaction*, New Delhi: Association of Indian Universities, p. 3.
6. P.K. Doraiswamy, 'The gains from industry-academia interaction', *Financial Daily from THE HINDU group of publications.*
7. Rao, B. Prasad & Subodh Bhargava, (2011). 'Academia-Industry Interactions-the Status, the Issues and the Future Road Map', *Frontiers in Science and Technology: Abstracts of Plenary Sessions,* at the 98th Indian Science Congress, January 3-7.
8. *Report of Symposium.* Introduction, Research Park in the 21st Century, "Understanding Research, Science and Technology Parks: Global Best Practices", p. 32, National Academies Press, Washington, DC US Economic Development Administration 2006.

9. Weenen Hans van, (2000). "*Towards a vision of a sustainable university*", International Journal of Sustainability in Higher Education, Vol. 1 No. 1 MCB University Press, pp. 20-34.
10. NCURA (National Council of University Research Administrators and Industrial Research Institute). 2006. "Guiding Principles for University-Industry Endeavors: Report of a Joint Project of the National Council of University Research Administrators and the Industrial Research Institute, USA." NCURA, Washington, DC.
11. OECD (Organization for Economic Co-operation and Development). 2010. "Innovation Vouchers." OECD Policy Brief, OECD, Paris. http://www.oecd.org/innovation/policyplatform/48135973.pdf
12. Perkmann, M., and K. Walsh. 2007. "University-Industry Relationships and Open Innovation: Towards a Research Agenda." International Journal of Management Reviews 9 (4): 259–80.

Reflection - 7

Relevance of Coaching Institutions

The Journey

Long back there was a trend of home tuitions. Parents of school children, who were weak in studies, especially in Maths, Science and English, engaged a tutor to come home and teach the child for an hour or so daily or may be thrice a week; he/she was paid a reasonable amount depending on the number of subjects taught and time given. Gradually the trend changed and instead of the tutor visiting one home to another he/she started giving tuitions at his/her own place to approximately 2-3 children at a time. But slowly realizing the financial benefits from such private tuitions, the tutors gradually increased the number of students, studying at a time and charged fees per subject, according to the level of the class. Thus, gradually tuitions became a business and a means of earning a good amount of money along with some private job or one's education in a college or a university.

The trends and attitudes changed further culminating in intense interest of parents and business men who were impressed by the opportunity that since such private tuition can help school children, it can definitely also help and facilitate the college and university students, particularly those who along with higher education are preparing for competitions. Therefore, a new dimension was added to such private tuitions which gave rise to coaching centres, where 2-3 like-minded young educated adults started coaching 2-3 batches of at least 25-50 students. They started charging a good amount from the students which the parents were ready to pay as their children were getting good guidance and help from these centres and were scoring good marks. The amount raised through these centres was divided among the group of friends, who were equal partners in running the coaching business.

The goal and vision of minting money on a large scale took fire in business minded persons, who were running small centres. A genuine intention (for many) to provide a focussed guidance to school children appearing for boards and for young adults appearing for a number of competitions gave rise to what exists today viz. large scale, full-fledged coaching institutions with hundreds of students preparing for competitions and examinations and teachers earning a handsome amount of salary. The scope of coaching has also got extended to include enhancement of marketability of a person for a variety of professions in business and industry.

As per the 2011 population census, more than 480 million Indians are in the age group of 0-19 years.[1] They are a huge asset to our country as their youthful energy can be used to transform India from a developing to a developed country – the dream of Late A.P.J. Abdul Kalam, shared by millions. However we need a system whereby the potential of youth can be channelled for the good of the society. For this to happen, we require a holistic educational policy and infrastructure, which can meet the needs our large population, where no child is left behind or unattended. This sentiment mainly was the reason behind the growth of coaching classes. Today, a child's brilliance is measured from his scorecard and students who are unable to cope up with peer pressure are sometimes committing suicide. The idea of high school and college students also attending the coaching classes has penetrated deep into our society. But we hardly see anyone analysing the effectiveness of coaching institutes, let alone consider desirable changes in the educational policy due to the coaching experience.

Coaching is a subject to which little or no attention has been paid by educationists. In general it is fashionable to denounce coaching as detrimental to education. However the growth in coaching institutions makes one to sit up, take note and analyse the situation objectively. Coaching classes have become as important and necessary as schools these days. Rarely do we see a kid taking up something without the help of coaching— be it studying, learning a musical instrument or playing sports. Coaching classes are a trend in India and especially when it comes to the field of education. But important question is, are they just that — a trend? Or is our education system failing us and coaching institutes filling up the gap?

Coaching Centres: The Picture Today

To paraphrase Albert Einstein, *it takes a different kind of thinking to solve a problem than the kind of thinking which produced the problem.* Simply, "coaching" is the process of helping people to develop their capacity to think about things (such as problems, people, relationships, customers, products, services, the future) in new and creative ways so that they can accomplish what they really want to accomplish. Coaching has an enormously important role in building and sustaining great organizations and extraordinary workplaces. People who want to accomplish great things often get stuck along the way. Coaching helps people get un-stuck. An example of this is that while many leaders, executives, and managers in organizations seem to "know" intuitively what they need to do to move forward, few of them actually follow through because they're stuck in some way. Coaching helps people focus on the things that are contributing to their being stuck, and then move beyond these.

Coaching centers have enormously proliferated in our educational system. The ever-growing demand for professional education and aspiration to study in the top institutes has resulted in more and more students depending on coaching centers. These centers have established themselves and emerged as the reliable means of scoring high in the entrance tests, conducted by various institutions. With competition growing in all the sectors, there are a large number of coaching institutes, flourishing in every nook and corner of every big or small city. Some coaching centres have a number of branches, not only in the same city but in other cities as well. Full-fledged franchise system and multi-campus system have also been introduced.

Earlier, students were more inclined to self-study with manageably good marks. This trend seems to have gone for a toss with parents, teachers and students looking for just the best scores. Students now need to join coaching institutes to study extra and get those extra marks.

It is evident that peer and parental pressure have resulted in this state. The uncertainty in school education has led to the boom of tuitions/ coaching classes.

Coaching institutes have also become a new hub of entertainment. Students attend extra classes not only to improve their academic understanding but also to socialize. It has become the next in-thing to join such institutes. Also, it is a sort of networking that helps a student exchange information, notes, books, etc. Education given in schools and colleges in India now needs a helping hand, available in coaching centers. As students are not satisfied with the education given in universities and colleges, they feel the need to go out and look for some extra help. But it sometimes leads to a change in their attitude towards studies; it makes them sluggish as they become excessively dependent on outside help. Amidst all the extra coaching and socializing, they tend to forget that it is they who have to ultimately work hard and thus score good marks.

Coaching System: Picture in Korea

Tutoring services are growing all over the globe, from Ireland to Hong Kong and even in suburban strip malls in California and New Jersey. Sometimes called shadow education systems, they mirror the mainstream system, offering after-hours classes in every subject—for a fee. But nowhere have they achieved the market penetration and sophistication of hagwons in South Korea, where private tutors now outnumber school teachers. Viewed up close, this shadow system is both exciting and troubling. It promotes striving and innovation among students and teachers alike, and it has helped South Korea become an academic superpower. But it also creates a bidding war for education, delivering the best services to the richest, to say nothing of its psychological toll on students. Under this system, students essentially go to school twice, once during the day and then again at night at the tutoring academies. No doubt it is a ruthless grind.

Education is a serious matter for South Korea. The country invested heavily in education during the second half of the 20th century, and in 2010, spent 7.6% of its GDP on all levels of education – significantly more than the Organisation for Economic Cooperation and

Development (OECD) average of 6.3%. During that same year, South Korea spent 2.6% on tertiary education, a figure also above the OECD average of 1.6%. In 2009, spending on private tuition in South Korea was the highest as a proportion of GDP among OECD countries, and according to the Ministry of Education, South Koreans spent 19 trillion Won (US $17.9 billion) on private tuition in 2012. Overall, education accounted for nearly 12% of consumer spending in 2012 – a large amount of which went toward extra English classes.[2]

What's driving these levels of investment? As reported in *The Economist*, it's competition for college places: "Throughout their children's school years, the South Koreans spend an extraordinary amount preparing them for the brutally competitive day-long university entrance exam, the *suneung*." And exam preparation begins early. According to Statistics in Korea, four out of five primary school children receive private education, typically in cram schools known as *hagwon*. Private schooling in South Korea operates on an "industrial scale," with 75% of all South Korean children attending one of the country's 100,000 *hagwons*.[3]

The outcome of this huge investment in education has been high academic performers. South Korean students consistently rank at the top of the Programme for International Student Assessment (PISA) survey results in reading, mathematics, and science. South Korea is also one of the highest educated nations in the world; in 2011, 64% of its 25-34 year-old population had university degrees, more than in the OECD, and well above the average of 39% among OECD states. Entry to a top university has traditionally led to a prestigious, secure and well-paid job with the government, banks, or one of South Korea's *chaebol* – family-owned conglomerates such as Samsung and Hyundai. As such, it's no wonder that, "South Korea's zeal for education and individuals' desire to get into a prestigious university is higher than in any other country in the world," as Kim HyeSook, professor of education at Yonsei University in Seoul, recently explained to Bloomberg news. South Korean university graduates are also prepared to "queue" for coveted jobs, adding to their educational credentials and enduring unemployment until a job becomes available. Among the 5.4 million South Koreans aged 15-29 who are not working, 11% are preparing for professional exams.

Although they perform well on international tests, South Korean students' interest in school and satisfaction rate is low, relative to their peers in other OECD countries. According to the Korean Institute for Curriculum and Evaluation, this is because South Korean students learn to prepare for their university entrance exams, as opposed to learning for practical use or its own sake. More disturbingly, Statistics for Korea and the Ministry of Gender Equality and Family last year reported that worry over career and academic performance is the main reason youths aged 13-19 contemplate suicide. According to the report, suicide was the biggest cause of death among people aged 15-24 in 2011.[4]

Coaching System: Picture in India

Beyond schools, 20% at graduation level and 13% at post-graduation and above levels in India are availing private tuition. One out of every four students in India takes private tuition and in a couple of states more than three out of every four students, or over 75%, opt for it, according to a report by the National Sample Survey Office (NSSO). Taking private coaching classes individually or in a group, at home or at any other place, by a single or more tutors for different reasons has become a norm, the survey underlined. More students opting for private tuition reflects poorly on the quality of education in schools and colleges.

"In this survey it is noted that in states like Tripura (around 81%) and West Bengal (around 78%) majority of students were taking private coaching (combining school education and higher education), whereas at all-India level 1/4th of students were taking private coaching," the NSSO survey said. Even in Delhi, 32.2% of the male students and 36.6% of the female students at primary schools avail of private tuition, the NSSO survey showed.

"Private tuition is thriving because the education system in India has deteriorated over the last several years. While quality of teaching has gone down across verticals, the exam system remains the same. The outcome is obvious. Students and parents believe in supplementary education like coaching for passing an exam or cracking a competitive exam," said Pramod Maheshwari, chairman and managing director of Career Point Ltd., a listed coaching company based in Kota. He, however, found it difficult to believe that in Uttar Pradesh, the dependency on private tuition is low. According to the data, in Uttar Pradesh only 12.2% of male students are availing of tuition at primary level and 13.7% in upper primary level as against the national average of 23.1% and 28%, respectively. Similarly, only 15.8% of Uttar Pradesh students avail of coaching at graduation level and 9.5% at post-graduation and above levels are availing of private coaching against the national average of 20.3% and 13%, respectively. According to NSSO data, 20% of Indians pursuing degree courses and 13% pursuing postgraduate courses and above avail of private tuition.[5]

Private Coaching: The Negative Face

According to the National Sample Survey Organisation, around 7.1 crore Indian children attend some form of private coaching and 10 to 11 per cent of a family's budget is consumed by such tuitions. The private coaching industry is bigger than $ 40 billion. This is about the state GDP of Odisha. Kota is a burning example of this huge yet shadow education system. The $ 45-million dollar coaching industry in the city has led to the suicide of 57 young people in the last five years- seven students just last year i.e. 2016.

Research suggests that coaching in Kota well begins when the child is 13 years old. The child would never attend a regular school with playgrounds or read poems in a class. She will only undertake IIT/ medical college preparation classes. The creativity is killed before it blooms. The two-year cost (including tuition and living expenses) for parents could be around Rs. 6 lakh — India's average per capita annual income is about Rs. 86,000. Acceptance rates as low as 0.005 per cent (for IITs) leaves the unsuccessful students dejected and guilt-ridden, definitely an enormous psychological and emotional cost that the country is paying.

The question that needs to be answered is whether there is any benefit which justifies this cost? Does coaching add value to human capital, or is it merely a signalling device? If it adds value then the governments must encourage them. But if it's the latter, alternative means of signalling must be evolved given the terrible social cost. There is some evidence about its benefit. Pratham conducted a two-year randomised control trial and found that private tutoring in school (grade 3 or 4) did benefit students in mastering basic skills. But there is no systematic evidence which shows that coaching for entrance examinations to colleges leads to any significant increase in productivity. In India, due to a high number of applicants, entrance examinations brutally cast aside many.

If the coaching classes indeed contributed to human capital, then we should surely find IIT graduates taken coaching for long, excelling in their career significantly more than their un-coached counterparts (controlling for other things). Unfortunately there is no evidence to show this. Although there is no evidence to show the contrary either, it is not difficult to imagine the need of coaching merely as signalling. A World Bank publication (Dang and Rogers, 2008) theoretically explains that coaching institutions are not likely to add value to human capital. In fact, an increase in signalling efforts comes at the cost of human capital — in Kota, formal education for the IIT/medical college aspirant is offered in dummy schools which lack well-rounded education. Entrance tests measure merely signalling value and therefore, coaching is not likely to increase students' human capital any more than self-practice does.

Now the question is what must be the policy response? Countries have varying responses to private coaching viz. ban (in Korea, Myanmar, Cambodia), regulate (in Hong Kong, Korea, Vietnam, Ukraine), ignore (in Nigeria, Sri Lanka, UK, Canada) or encourage (in Singapore, South Africa, Tanzania). Banning has been unsuccessful either due to weak implementation (Myanmar, Cambodia) or because of powerful interest groups (Korea). Banning doesn't make sense in India too. Regulation could be useful. But India has weak enforcement infrastructure and a highly inelastic demand for coaching. Therefore, alternative signalling mechanisms must be explored. Many elite universities around the world often select students on the basis of their overall intelligence and performance in schools. For many, exams act as a process to eliminate non-serious applicants, but don't determine their selection. Selection happens through a rigorous process of considering several factors — grades, recommendations, interviews, motivation, extra-curricular activities. This means students must attend regular schools engaging with history, poetry, mathematics, debating and football. In such alternative systems, there is little that coaching institutions can do to terminate creativity of societies. If anything, they will turn themselves into good schools — and definitely more good schools are needed.[6]

Preference for Private Tuitions over College Tutorials

In India, about 40 percent of the total population does not have worthwhile assets for generation of income to support their minimum requirements for maintaining a decent standard of living. They are largely wage earners in the un-organized sector. The level of education, training and skills of the workforce determines the wages and salaries in the knowledge intensive economy. The quality education provider institutions have hardly offered any opportunities of learning to them, and this is the reason that they have lagged far behind in their contribution to productivity growth and economic development. The wide spread existence of such disparities across groups and regions gives rise to discontent and disturbance in harmonious relations between different sections of the society. One of the important implications is in respect of the fundamental right to education and also the Constitutional obligations of the state. These rights and obligations have been eclipsed under the growing influence of commercialization of education.

Most students, especially who attend government schools terminate their education on completion of +2 stages. A majority of them, therefore, need vocational preparation to enter the world of work. A large proportion of students, therefore, seek support of private institutions, which provide vocational training and offer job-oriented courseson commercial basis.

Despite the compulsory attendance factor in tutorials, also called 'doubt-solving classes' in Universities and colleges, students are making a beeline for private tuition classes shelling out a sum of Rs. 500 per month to Rs. 400 per hour. The demand for private tuitions is even more during the exam season. Students say that taking tuitions in tough subjects like maths, accounts, statistics, taxation and economics is imperative as the 50-minute period is not enough to tackle each and every student's problem. A final year student of Economics (Hons.) from Delhi College of Arts and Commerce, said: "The syllabus for Economics (Hons.) in second year is difficult with a heavy dose of Maths, and since there is no time to discuss problems in the class we are compelled to get help from private tuitions." While for many, private tuitions delivered in a structured and systematic manner is more useful than classroom teaching. The point to be noted here is that private coaching is perceived to be more structured and systematic as compared to classroom lectures.

A second year student of B.A. from Aurobindo College, Delhi said, "Private tutors are more competent and they give us personalized attention to help us to score well." Irregularity among teachers in college and inconvenient timings of college tutorials are some of the reasons cited for opting for private tuitions. "Students who live far from campus find tutorials a waste of time and while some end up missing the tutorials, others persuade their friends to put their proxy in attendance," accepted a student. A Lecturer from a reputed College in Delhi added that students are aware that a B.A. degree will not fetch them a job hence they take coaching for job-oriented courses like computers, CAT or foreign languages.

A survey conducted by ASSOCHAM Social Development Foundation has found that falling teaching standards and fear of poor performance in school, college and national level assessments drive urban Indian middle class parents to seek private tuitions for their school going children. The report states that "The origin of tuitions lies in bad classroom teaching… if a student feels the need for tuitions, it means that the teacher has not been able to do justice in the class". In another damning observation made by Mr. D.S. Rawat, Secretary General of Assocham, "Most schools conveniently pass the ball back to parents, telling them to engage private tutors. This is a serious failure in the education system".[7]

The survey highlights that parents spend as much as 1/3 of their monthly income on private tuitions and that an astonishing 97% of students in the surveyed cities were taking additional tuition classes in at least one subject (98% in Math followed closely by Science subjects like Chemistry and Physics). In urban India, the last few decades has witnessed a boom in private tuitions, group tuitions and tutorial classes which have now become one of the fastest-growing enterprises in India. The industry is estimated to be a multimillion rupee industry which has grown at 40%-45% in the last 5 years. Assocham estimates that as many as 30 million students in major cities are attending tuition classes of one kind or the other with the demand for tuitions starting as early as primary school.

Thus, concluding from the above discussion on preference for private tuitions and coaching classes, it can be said that students have always found private lectures to be more structured and systematic. The higher education institutes who have always promised quality education and who have always wanted to be pathfinders for its students are actually falling short of standards. Normal classroom teaching is not preparing students overall in different skills required by them in the world of work. Moreover, the courses that are being offered in universities and higher education institutes are not preparing students vocationally so that they can be helped to be independent, the need of every individual today. And so they are looking for coaching institutes to prepare them for vocational courses.

Coaching Institutes: Boon or bane

Today, coaching classes have become an important part of every student's life. While the debate about the importance of these classes continues, one cannot deny the fact that coaching classes do come with a set of advantages, especially when it comes to preparing for the competitive exams. The purpose of competitive exams is to screen students with the right aptitude for a said profession. Therefore simply mugging up the study material may not prove to be useful; it's important to have a strategy in place. Thus a well-charted plan is the need of the day, and this brings us to one of the important advantages of enrolling in a coaching class.

Some of the advantages that the students' community get in coaching classes include guidance from the best brains in the field and use of technology, which helps in understanding the concepts better. Children receive either individual care or are put into classes with smaller student-to-teacher ratio. Coaching classes provide training for specific entrance examinations, which eventually reduces the load on the students and gives them guidance at one place.

- ***Guidance***

Proper guidance is vital. Coaching centers have experienced and qualified teachers, who have been in the business long enough to understand and analyze test patterns and identify the need of the day. Their responsibility does not end with just teaching the curriculum. They provide relevant, exam-oriented suggestions, notes and handouts, which help students utilize their time optimally. They provide guidance to students on crucial matters like how to study, what to study, etc. One is familiarized with question paper patterns, frequently asked questions, important chapters and topics, etc. Tuition centers cover the syllabus in detail saving time and energy of students in running around, collecting notes and references. Coaching institutes can act mentors for every pupil individually which is not possible for teachers in schools and colleges. Extra tuitions drill students with befitting information that proves opportune for entrance or other competitive tests. Moreover, they encourage pupils to discuss their problems and doubts more openly.

Education Counsellor Jayanti Ghosh feels, "Coaching classes can play a supportive role. They guide and orient the students in the right direction by familiarizing them with the range of content they must cover for the exam, help them develop their skills and abilities by providing essential study material; and mock tests with model papers; and assessments."

- ***Exam equipped***

Sudeshna Mukherjee, Language Head, PT Education, Indore, says, "Unlike earlier exams, competitive entrance exams such as CAT undergo frequent pattern changes. The objective is to surprise the takers. Under such circumstances, it makes sense to attach oneself to a training center, since they prepare one to face varying patterns with ease through well-designed mock tests and the guidance of expert faculty." These tests can give ample practice as they teach prompt response to tricky questions and management of time.

- ***Ambience***

Coaching classes create the right environment. Mukherjee mentions, "Meeting fellow aspirants at these institutes can be a great confidence booster." Though self-study is essential, preparing without being in touch with the rest of the world may prove to be a huge drawback. It helps to interact and network with like-minded people. Discussing relevant topics and exam trends might help gain insights which otherwise one might have been deprived of.

Drawbacks

But is the coaching class culture causing more harm than good? The rise of coaching classes has jeopardized the schooling culture. Many students don't pay attention in the class and bunk them as they always have coaching classes to teach them again. They are wasting valuable resources and time in the process. It is also a big blow for the motivation of school teachers. Most good teachers have now left their school jobs and entered the lucrative business of coaching, where they get better pay and autonomy too. It has led to a decrease in understanding of a subject as the coaching classes pay less attention on concepts and more on problem-solving. There is no scope for inquisitiveness as students are encouraged to accept things given in the textbooks. Mathematical "magic tricks" – a section common in all coaching class study material are taught to students without making them understand the reason behind the *magic*.

Coaching institutes leave no time for extra-curricular activities. After school, students straight away head to the coaching classes, where an already fatigued mind learns less than its ability. Many times, students are caught chatting over the phone and listening to music in the class because of stress. There has been an increase in the cases of headache, neck ache, obesity, eye-related issues in students because of their hectic lifestyle. A startling report says that 41% children (under 18 years) in India need optical correction. That population is estimated to be around 200 million.

Coaching classes cause a big blow to the financial status of families. The private coaching institutions exploit the prevailing excessive demand for education and operate with profit motives; they charge high fees. The reasons for demand can be two-fold viz. the inability of the government, universities and higher education institutions to provide quality education to all those who need or desire it. It is here that coaching institutions find a fertile ground for undertaking their activities on a commercial basis.

All the big names in the field of IIT coaching charge more than a lakh per year for their two years classroom course. It excludes the charges for food and lodging if a student from outside the city opts for their facilities. The National Commission on Enterprises in the Unorganised Sector (NCEUS) has pointed out that going by consumer expenditure data, 78% of Indians are forced to manage with Rs. 20 or less per day – indicating three-fourths of the population live in poverty. So, by those numbers, coaching fees take the salt of food for any average family. But names like Anand Kumar of the Super 30 fame cannot be ignored, where he teaches the underprivileged students of the society and has got excellent success track record in IIT JEE.

A large number of students, who do not join colleges/ universities as regular students, are allowed to appear as external/ non-collegiate students at degree level examinations. Many of them attend coaching centers, which charge high fees. Correspondence course institutions have taken almost similar advantage. The Government's failure to fulfill its mandatory obligations of making adequate provisions for quality education, commensurate with the requirements for quality teaching and learning, is chiefly responsible for encouraging commercial activities in education. As education is profitable, socially and economically, parents and their wards have little options. They are, therefore, easily exploited either by paying high un-economic costs of education or by foregoing quality education, which in any case creates all forms of disparities.

Some people feel that coaching institutes are only a means of making money. They believe that education in India has become a business for many. According to them, it is a deal that these institutes make with the students to help them in clearing an exam. Coaching centers charge high fees from students promising to prepare them for competitive tests and for getting them into their dream college. But both parents and students are ready to bear the costs as they think it is worth it if a child can really get in the desirable course and college and build a successful career.

Private coaching institutes in India have created an out-of-school learning system which is based on rote learning and practice tests. It does not focus on fundamental learning, building of concepts or creating a free mind which makes students think out of the box. It restricts students as it is a restrictive education system based on past exam papers.

Annually, one million students flock to Kota, a city in the state of Rajasthan, which is also the hub of coaching institutes to crack the prestigious engineering and medical entrance exams. Coaching institutes in Kota have tied up with schools who allow the coaching institute students to completely skip class 11 and 12, and attend only the institute classes for 8-10 hours per day. Students aspiring to crack engineering entrances are only being taught physics, chemistry and maths. The ones aspiring to become doctors are taught chemistry and biology, along with physics. After studying day and night for two years, some of the students due to rote learning and practice based learning methodology clear the entrance exams to get into IITs & medical schools. Such critical two years of a student is just fixed on 'lousy' learning methodology of coaching institutes. More importantly, such students skip important subjects like English and other vocational subjects which are taught in school. Additionally, there is a huge difference between the learning environment at school and these coaching institutes.

In general, coaching institutions of education are not accepted and approved by the society, particularly in countries like India, which have a democratic polity. But, inequality of opportunities and provisions for educational services contribute to inter-personal, inter-regional and inter-generational disparities of all kind. These perpetuate socio-economic disparities and hamper national development. Moreover, India's long history, tradition and culture of imparting free knowledge and training have put pious obligations on the duty conscious society for providing worthwhile education.

The socio-economic benefits over the entire span of working life accrue more to educated and trained persons and therefore, attempts are made by students and their parents to obtain good education at even high private costs. The demand for various types and levels of courses is much higher than the available places/seats for learning in creditable institutions. To meet excess demand, coaching institutions have been established in almost every part of country, these institutions have received social support. A lack of effective mechanism to identify and discourage poor institutions that are offering coaching has created an environment for mushrooming of such institutions.

In Kota there are some coaching institutes which teach the whole day, at Higher Secondary level and also prepare students for competitive exams. Thus, a single class takes care of both. Practical are skipped or taken up in a haphazard manner. Students' time and energy is saved. However, their overall exposure to schools is missing. This system is marring the students of the school culture which is very important for their development.

Thinking about the Solution!

After the above discussion on the increasing need and necessity of coaching institutes, it remains a food for thought as to what is actually lacking in our universities and higher education institutes that the need and value of coaching institutes is increasing among students and teachers. As discussed before, these institutes are offering guidance in different subjects in systematic form which is not available in universities. Everyday it's the same monotonous format and lectures being offered to students. One alternative is that both universities and colleges change their style of teaching and learning or the other alternative is to begin outsourcing whereby the teachers from some good coaching institutes and elsewhere take lectures in universities and colleges (with extra fees). The teaching and learning in universities and higher education institutes need to be rescheduled according to the needs of students and demands of the educational world today. Skill training and preparing students for vocational courses have to become an important part of university teaching.

Improving the funding and infrastructure of the existing schools is one step. Timely recruitment of teachers can be another. It will instil the faith of society in government schools. Schools with fewer teachers should be provided with video lectures made on subject curriculum by experts, and this should follow the line of NPTEL videos for engineering. Frequent inspection of the schools and suspension for negligence of duty should be routine. Breaking the madness for engineering & medical professions and concentrating on physical education, arts, humanities and entrepreneurship is another important step. We should reduce the economic and social gap between rural and urban areas in India. It is also imperative to provide incentives to online-based coaching classes so that students can choose their time of reading and don't have to get tired from travelling from one place to another.

According to a report published by IIT-Guwahati (the conducting body for IIT-JEE 2016), 52.4% of students who qualified for the IIT entrance exam in 2016 never took any coaching for entrance exam preparation and studied on their own. Such statistics clearly prove that you do not necessarily need to join a coaching centre to clear entrance exams and achieve success. This should bring back our attention to improving the learning environment in school which can clearly allow a student to learn and even clear such entrance exams.[8]

Many Indian school teachers make hefty amounts of money by providing tuitions outside school. Lots of teachers are not doing their job in the schools. And such behaviour is due to very low and stagnant salaries of school teachers in India. We need to understand the importance of teachers and their efforts. They need to be paid at par with people in other professions in the market. Only then will schools have the authority to regulate such behaviour of teachers. But as they don't pay well, they don't care and more importantly, the school authorities do not care about what is being taught. As they have now agreed that it's not their job to educate students, it is the responsibility of private tuition and coaching.

The entire system, along with all the stakeholders, which includes the schools, teachers, students, parents have passed on the responsibility of delivering 'education' to coaching institutes. Clearly, they no longer believe that school education is important. It's the students of our country, whose aspirations, dreams and eagerness to learn is being crushed down by such beliefs. We need to act and bring back the confidence in our school education system. Schooling is a fundamental way of learning. We have created a powerful ecosystem to deliver education but we are trying to clear another parallel system of private coaching which fails to deliver quality education.

Another effective suggestion is that instead of coaching institutes the schools should run such a programme after retraining of existing teachers and having new teachers. Another mode is that the school itself runs a coaching programme which is completely independent of the regular conduct of classes. The head of this programme will only report to the management and work in collaboration with the Principal. They may have dedicated teachers in this programme and school teachers after proper orientation and training.

Any of these programmes will have the infrastructure of the school at their disposal and thus cost much less than comparable programmes elsewhere. At the same time the ambience could be much better. This will supplement the revenue and resources of the school for further development and higher standards. The culture of the competitive exams namely higher level of understanding and application will also trickle down to the regular programmes of the school. A companion activity could be Extension classes in subjects like Language Communication, Yoga, Life Skills, Music, Dancing, foreign language etc. which will enrich the student's experiences; it will make the institute share its expertise and infrastructure with the community.

Our Experience

We conclude the Reflection on *Relevance of Coaching Institutions* by a report on Status Survey carried out by us in Eastern U.P. titled **'Rationale of Coaching Centres for Youth: A Status Survey of Eastern U.P.'**

A desire arose in the mind of the researchers to give a little more strength to the above facts and opinions either that quoted by ASSOCHAM or for that matter what the Delhi university professors observed. The researchers wanted to investigate and validate the above conclusions in the state of Uttar Pradesh with students from different colleges and universities all over U.P., especially the Eastern U.P. The researchers made an attempt to explore and survey the reasons behind the students for joining coaching centres and what difference did they feel in teaching pattern of coaching and that of a college and a university. Thus, an effort was made to explore the attitude and mind set of students preparing for competitive examinations in different coaching institutes in Lucknow and other districts of Uttar Pradesh, towards college teaching and teaching in coaching classes.

Sample & Methodology

The present study was done in two phases. First a pilot study was done with 100-120 students from Lucknow city and then the main study was conducted with approximately 200-300 students from different parts and cities of Uttar Pradesh.

Pilot Study

Firstly, with the help of self-made questionnaire an opinion survey was done with students taking coaching in different coaching centres in Lucknow city.

An **opinion survey** is an inquiry into public opinion conducted by interviewing some participants from a larger population, where each of those selected is chosen randomly (entirely by chance). Trained interviewers ask questions of people chosen at random from the population being measured. Responses are given, and interpretations are made based on the results. It is important in a random sample that everyone in the population being studied has an equal chance of participating. Otherwise, the results could be biased and, therefore, not representative of the population. Representative samples are chosen in order to make generalizations about a particular population being studied. Polls tell us what proportion of a population has a specific viewpoint. They do not explain why respondents believe as they do or how to change their minds. This is the work of social scientists and scholars. Polls are simply a measurement tools that tell us how a population thinks and feels about any given topic. Two of the most common ways in which public opinion polls are conducted are telephone and face-to-face interviews. Other methods include mail, online, and self-administered surveys.[9]

For the pilot study approximately 100-120 students were randomly selected from different coaching institutes in Lucknow preparing for competitions and were surveyed. The researcher herself administered the self-made questionnaire and face to face interviews were taken of few students. Building a rapport and talking with students on an issue gives them an open opportunity to share their true feelings. The responses of the students to different questions were studied in detail. A very high degree of correlation was found between the opinions of the students in their reasons for preferring coaching over college or university teaching.

The Main Study

The researchers wanted to explore and validate the above findings in Lucknow city with large sample group and with students not only in Lucknow but those taking coaching in different towns and cities in Uttar Pradesh especially in Eastern U.P. Thus, the main part of the study was conducted with the help of the students pursuing teacher training course who helped in data collection from coaching institutes in different districts. An orientation was given to these few students who were selected for data collection. Approximately 250-300 students from different coaching institutes were interviewed and surveyed on a self-made questionnaire with questions related with the relevance of coaching institutes in comparison to classes in university or colleges. The questionnaire was prepared both in English and Hindi language for the clear understanding by the students. The students ranged between age group 17years to 28 years. Students who were surveyed have been preparing for Polytechnic exam, Civil Services, S.S.C. exam, Banking, M.B.A. Medicals and other competitions. The students belonged to districts like Gorakhpur, Lucknow, Deoria, Khushinagar, Siddharth-nagar, Ambedkarnagar, Sultanpur, Amethi, Barabanki, Kanpur, Sitapur, Fiazabad, Lakhimpur Khiri, Hardoi and Azamgarh areas of Eastern U.P.

Students at the intermediate level and taking coaching to crack some competitive exam and others in the university or college pursuing their under graduation or post-graduation, took part in the survey. There were other group of students who have completed their education and are preparing for competition since last one to two years. The same methodology was followed as in the Pilot study. An opinion survey and few interviews with open ended questions were asked from the students and opinion taken.

Observations and Findings

The responses of the students to different question related with coaching and college teaching could be categorized under the following categories:

1. Quality of teachers
2. Quality of teaching
3. Teaching techniques
4. Importance of college teaching and teaching in coaching centres

A qualitative analysis was done of the responses of the students for each question. Some important findings have been discussed here.

Majority of the students preferred going to coaching in comparison to the college. However there were few students who preferred going to both college and coaching. They gave reasons like they basically go to college for the attendance and degree while they go to coaching for in-depth knowledge which will ultimately help them in preparing for their competitions. Students feel that an atmosphere of group study in coaching centres is beneficial for them as it helps them and give them opportunities for group discussion, discussing extra questions which they normally cannot do in their colleges or university atmosphere. The students feel that they are taught in a much more organized manner in coaching institutes as compared to college institutions; in colleges and universities there is more time wastage but in coaching the teaching and preparation is more focussed and organized. However, some students who preferred going to college or university feel that in colleges they get basic fundamental knowledge which helps them understand the basics of the subject.

"Good teachers with good teaching techniques", "more knowledge in less time", "coaching is more time saving as compared to college or university teaching where a lot of time is wasted"; these were few of the opinions given by students. Also students said that in coaching they get complete practical knowledge which is important and useful to crack competitions that they don't get in college classrooms. Some students expressed that there is nothing special except this that in coaching teachers teach more enthusiastically and systematically as compared to teachers in a college.

As mentioned above students belonged to different districts of U.P. It was really a mind opening finding that students, either coming from good financial status or from poor families and belonging to any part of U.P. had almost same opinion and feelings about the college teaching and teachers and their opinion about coaching centres. Like for example, most of the students expressed that they find teachers in coaching centres more approachable, friendly, understanding and motivating as compared to those in colleges and universities. Students find teachers in coaching more regular in taking classes and more responsible towards their work in comparison to teachers teaching in colleges and universities. Teachers in coaching centres are more accountable as compared to teachers in colleges and universities. They opined that in coaching institutes teachers daily take classes and every class is important so ***'we cannot afford to miss it'***. Also teachers consider themselves responsible towards what they teach. They are committed to it but in colleges mostly teachers teach just to complete the syllabus i.e. just as a formality. Many times they are absent or they do not take class. They also have indifferent attitude towards the students i.e. they are least bothered whether students understand the concept or not. Teachers in coaching motivate the students and build enthusiasm in them.

As far as quality and methodology of teaching are concerned majority students find teaching much better in coaching classes as compared to teaching in college and or university classrooms. Students feel that in coaching they get a systematic way of explanation of concepts through diagrams, live examples, case studies and power point presentations. Also printed notes are provided; teachers in coaching do not only provide content from books but extra knowledge is also provided to the students that improves their General Knowledge. Only few teachers in colleges and universities sincerely use and show interest in teaching through power points, examples, discussions and brainstorming sessions etc.

In coaching, students feel free to ask questions and satisfy their curiosity. Coaching also gives ample time for revision and recapitulation of the content taught. One important point that has been emphasized by majority of the students was that in coaching classes they are provided with short tricks or short cut methods to solve problems which are very useful for competitive exams but in normal, regular college classroom teaching, no such tricks or methods are provided to the students.

Each and every student in coaching class is made to participate in Group Discussions and mock interviews so that they are well prepared for higher levels of competitive exams. Students also opined that colleges have more facilities and technologies available with them like projectors and other multimedia techniques but unfortunately teachers are very resistant in using these technologies either because they don't want to or they don't know how to use them, also because they are not technology friendly. Students also feel that coaching centres put more emphasis on problem solving techniques and they do their best to inculcate problem solving skills in students but unfortunately college and university classroom teaching lacks this strategy.

A student said**, "The college administration should learn from the coaching administration so that there is improvement in the education system."** No matter how the student expressed it he meant overall that the colleges and universities need to renew their teaching strategies and attitude towards the students. In coaching along with teaching, students are also given vocational and educational guidance and facilitation in choosing subjects for further competitions. This brings forth the issue that our universities and colleges need to have a cell in Guidance and Counselling so that students can be provided career counselling.

Students feel that they develop self-confidence through studying in coaching. They feel that all their doubts and questions are answered very patiently in a coaching as compared to college classrooms. A unique point that came up is that students feel that in coaching all the students are given equal attention but in college only students who are good in studying are paid attention to. It means that students feel a partial attitude of teachers in college classrooms.

Many students emphasized that coaching also develops communication skills, studying habits, understanding power, good manners, discipline, sincerity and an ability to understand one's own weaknesses. There is more emphasis on mind development. Students studying in coaching find themselves different from college students in knowledge and overall personality aspects. The coaching atmosphere gives the students opportunities to express their views, for open discussions and to build their confidence. Teaching and discussions in coaching centres by the teachers make the students better problem solvers. They are given better problem solving techniques. They become more independent and improve their communication and interpersonal skills. They also build better management and interview skills and become more confident to face interviews in future.

The finding of this survey brought forward the realization and an important question as to why students are more inclined towards studying in coaching centres. They bunk their classes, miss their college and attend coaching classes for hours. Why? It is a very pertinent question to analyse. The present exploration through survey technique has brought forward eye opening findings. Students no matter from which district or part of state they belong feel almost the same for college teaching, teachers and college and university atmosphere and prefer going to coaching centres. Few students have expressed that both college and coaching are important because there are certain things that we can get in college only and others in a coaching centre. **"We go to coaching so that we can reach our goal which is not possible in a college or a university." "We don't dislike going to college, it's just that we are time bound and have to prepare for competitions. If similar teaching is done in a college, we will prefer it more and save our time."** Mentorship is required in today's system of college education so that students can openly discuss their weak points.

It may be appreciated that a university/college is best suited to provide academic knowledge to student, while a coaching institute can best provide marketable skills. Hence a combination of the college/ university and coaching institute can provide marketable skills as well as the needed academic background, which can form the basis for acquisition of newer marketable skills. Thus, a university/college can provide the study material and evaluation system of the academic component of a course (e.g. B.Com Applied). The coaching institute can provide the marketable skills and the evaluation system. Thus a student will get a degree (B.Com Applied Academic) from the University and a certificate/diploma from the coaching institute. The recognition of a coaching institution by the university/college also defacto provides a regulating mechanism. The value placed on a degree by all concerned provides sustainability to the system.

Conclusion

Thus, we see that coaching has become important because of the relatively poor teaching in schools, colleges and universities. One mode is that school and colleges open up their own coaching institutes. No country has all the answers. But in an information-driven global economy, a few truths are becoming universal. Children need to know how to think critically in maths, reading and science; and learn how to adapt, since they will be doing it all their lives. These demands require that schools change, too—or the free market may do it for them.

We all know that it is a knowledge era and a world of competition. Normal, regular and old fashioned way of classroom teaching methodology by teachers is of no help for students who have to face tough written and oral competitions in future. Colleges can very easily integrate teaching of the syllabus and competitive examination with proper guidance for group discussions and interviews. Maths, Economics and Commerce syllabus specially has to be made more competition oriented like it should help students to prepare for Banking, SSC. Exams etc.

However, at the same time the negative side of these coaching systems has to be taken care of. It cannot be denied that directly and indirectly the coaching institutions are putting undue pressure on the students and that is taking toll on their lives. It is also becoming a source of financial burden on parents who have to pay heavy amount for their wards for regular education as well for their coaching. Also an important question to ponder is if after so costly and time taking coaching a student is not selected and fails to clear the competition, then what? Is the student also being guided and counselled and being empowered to face such failures in life and stand again for the next attempt? For sure it is now the need of the hour that a strong step is taken to bring a balance in the financial crunch of regular education and that being given by the coaching institutes and to improve the quality of education especially higher education and to make it more competition oriented.

Last but not the least at the end of the day, irrespective of whether one attends a coaching class or not, it is the effort that will fetch the kind of results one desires. As Ghosh briefly puts it, "The coaching class does not determine success, the student's hard work does. They cannot create abilities and skills that the student does not possess or to a limited extent only, nor can they study on behalf of the students." Ultimately, scoring mainly depends on student's calibre. At the time when there were no coaching centres, students still cleared examinations only by self-study and focus. Even today, students may not feel the need of extra help if they believe in sheer hard work and tenacious determination; however some guidance is always helpful. Coaching makes a good student better.

Suggestions

At the end there are few suggestions that if implemented can go a long way to improve the higher education to a great extent.

1. The formal education system should be made more interesting, job oriented and nearer to life.
2. Coaching should be a recognized activity of the college or a university probably by a wing directly responsible to the Principal or the Vice Chancellor.
3. The administrative and financial rules should also be flexible for this purpose.
4. A separate director for this activity should be appointed.
5. The use of outside resources including teacher should be made liberally. Teaching in collaboration with similar units and industry should be explored.
6. Coaching for university examinations and competitive examinations should not be mixed.

7. As a policy it will be wise to develop a syllabus which integrates the requirements of the university as well as competitive examinations and employment in business/ industry.
8. Teachers in the coaching institutes should also engage themselves in research work to keep alive.
9. Personality development should be undertaken and must be an integral and mandatory part of higher education system.

References

This chapter is based on several readings including the following websites

Specific References

1. http://censusindia.gov.in/Census_And_You/age_structure_and_marital_status.aspx
2. http://monitor.icef.com/2014/01/high-performance-high-pressure-in-south-koreas-education-system/
3. http://www.koreaherald.com/view.php?ud=20170109000747
4. http://monitor.icef.com/2014/01/high-performance-high-pressure-in-south-koreas-education-system/
5. http://www.livemint.com/Politics/Dk8ry9VQkyRXcsJVHp9aNJ/Private-tuition-outside-schools-colleges-thrives-in-India.html
6. http://indianexpress.com/article/opinion/columns/shadow-education-private-coaching-kota-private-tuition-2859563/
7. http://assocham.org/newsdetail.php?id=4953
8. https://timesofindia.indiatimes.com/home/education/news/52-who-passed-IIT-JEE-relied-on-self-study-75-from-cities/articleshow/53818944.cms
9. http://media.gallup.com/muslimwestfacts/pdf/pollingandhowtouseitr1-dreveng.pdf

General References

Soni, R., M.S. Sodha, (2016): *Relevance of Coaching Institutions,* University News: A Weekly Journalof Higher Education, 54 (12), March 21-27 pp. 5-9.

Soni, R., M.S. Sodha, (2009):*Flexible Perception of Quality in Higher Education and Quality in the Light of available Inputs and Priorities,* University News: A Weekly Journal of Higher Education, 47 (50), 14-20, pp. 1-9.

https://www.toppr.com/bytes/life-coaching-classes/

http://www.wsj.com/articles/SB10001424127887324635904578639780-253571520

https://professorjee.wordpress.com/2015/08/17/role-of-coaching-centers-and-worst-condition-of-education-at-govt.-schools-and-colleges-in-karachi/

http://educationtimes.com/index.aspx?page=article&secid=69&conid=20100514201005141648047326913 5c1c

http://educationtimes.com/index.aspx?page=article&secid=69&conid=20100514201005141648047326913 5c1c

https://www.youthkiawaaz.com/2017/02/school-vs-coaching-institutes-time-to-revive-indian-schooling-system/

Reflection - 8

Indiscipline in Universities

Introduction

There is a widespread concern about the lack of discipline on our university and college campuses. Disturbances created by students and the presence of the police to deal with them have become common today. Campus disturbances take different forms. They manifest themselves in the form of deterioration of academic pursuit, use of unfair methods like cheating in examinations, politicization in various forms and pressure group activities. The increasing menace of indiscipline needs to be controlled if we want to maintain our campuses as true citadels of learning.

Our formal system of education remains confined to the four walls of a school or college. It is tied down with text books and examinations. Even then the books are unread package and examinations totally unreliable. The courses of study are so framed that the students are not equipped with any productive skills. Whatever education they receive cuts them off from their natural and social environment. They become aliens to their own community. They lose faith in their life itself and all this forms the genesis for indiscipline in universities.

Indiscipline in Universities

In disciplined behaviour of students, non-teaching employees and to a lesser extent teachers is a disturbing phenomenon on most of the university campuses. It results in considerable deterioration of performance in all spheres of activity at the university.

While the incidence of violence and indiscipline could be seen as symptomatic of a deeper malaise within the larger social system (the macrocosm) as well as within the university system (the microcosm) as a whole, they have been occasioned by a variety of deficiencies in the administrative, academic, and managerial aspects of the university system. The lacunae in university administration and teaching have given occasion for entry of forces and organizations outside the university to encroach on and usurp functions that should properly fall within the purview of university administrations and thereby serve as opportunities for such external forces to recruit new members, mobilize students for protests and demonstrations, and use them as instruments for enlarging the party revenues and activities. Since violence and indiscipline in the universities have multiple causes, they require multi-dimensional solutions that will need re-thinking on such critical areas as methods of conflict resolution, introducing courses that have a practical orientation especially for arts degree students, providing more opportunities for women participation in student councils, counselling services at intra-departmental level, demanding accountability and transparency in affairs of student bodies, seeking viable alternatives to the policy of having residential campuses, introducing minimum levy for higher education, tight security and surveillance of student activism, and meaningful participation of students in the management of universities.

State of Indiscipline

- ***Students***

The university is a subsystem of the society and hence reflects its values and norms of behaviour is not an alibi for the present state of indiscipline in the universities; however it has to be kept in mind for an appreciation of the genesis of indiscipline in the campus. Self-indulgence, craze for acquisition and display of power and money, absence of moral values and adoption of easy means to achieve the desired ends; characterize the ethics of a significant part of society. The media for mass communication have not only helped at the rapid growth of such an ethic, but have made deviations from normally accepted behaviour not only acceptable, but indeed desirable.

Indiscipline at individual level of students usually manifests itself in absenteeism, bullying, ragging, eve teasing and other unsocial means at the examinations. On a collective level there is a small hard core of students; usually having political connections, which engages in pressure tactics and violence; this core is able to muster the support of other students, at will. Most of the students in the hard core have political ambitions and work for recognition as aggressive student leaders, with a large following. Often these students use coercion, force or occasionally bribes to monopolize selected contractual and supply work of the university, to the de facto exclusion of all other competition; they also try with varying degrees of success, to influence the recruitment, admission and examination processes for financial or other considerations. Many times such students also have de facto control of university, hostels, enabling them to harbour indiscipline and criminal activity; they also have other residents of choice and deny residence to official allottees. In some cases indiscipline in the university campus is caused by the students in associated degree colleges and/or neighbouring universities due to the coupling between the two systems.

The violent activities on the campus by the hard core students, the inter gang warfare and intimidation of persons, engaged in their normal work, sometimes creates an atmosphere of terror in the university and also the city, because these activities are by no means confined to the campus alone.

A serious aspect of student indiscipline is the use of unfair means on a large scale by the students in the examinations; the associated criminal activity is intimidation and occasional physical assault on the invigilating faculty members and examiners. Staff members connected with examinations are also subjected to bribes, threats and beating by students or others on their behalf.

More often than not the aggressive elements in the leadership of students, employees and teachers are linked, often as youth, student, worker, cultural and other wings of political parties, to the political machine of the city/state; links to a common machine give rise to strong cross linkage between the three groups. The fact that the appointment of the Vice Chancellor is many times a politicized act also reinforces machinations of political nature in the university.

- ***Non-Teaching Employees***

The universities suffer to different degrees from indiscipline of non-teaching employees. The employees may be frequently absent from duty, indifferent and discourteous and using pressure tactics to achieve immediate ends; the competing unions only make the position worse by taking more and more militant postures. While some of these characteristics develop as a natural reaction to the environment in the campus, a desire for dominance in appointments, processing of disciplinary cases and distribution of goodies seems to be the prime mover.

- ***Teachers***

Some teachers who serve as role model for many students indulge in indiscipline and often flagrant violation of university culture, norms and rules. Irregularity in engaging classes, indifference in teaching and evaluation related work, intrigues, occupation with militant trade union style activities, using students to further self-interest, private tuition/ coaching and running business, even in normal university working hours, are some of the manifestations of indiscipline amongst teachers.

Genesis

- ***Students***

The genesis of student indiscipline lies in the state of universities, the academic programmes offered by them and the facilities available to undertake the programmes. The academic programme is devoid of challenge and does not require much effort to undertake it; even this programme is not offered in a professional manner. The facilities for academic work, sports, co-curricular activities and residence are poor; the teachers and staff of the university are at best indifferent to problems of individual nature. The absence of variety makes studies monotonous. Most of the academic programmes are not related to employment and the studies have little to look forward to after studies. In such an environment the students have plenty of motivation and time to indulge in activities bordering on or amounting to indiscipline.

A single fact which has contributed most to the nuisance value of the pressure groups is the fact that a grievance at individual/small group/

courteous level is neither heard properly nor receives attention, but the same or similar grievance, championed by a pressure group is promptly heard and attended to, despite the arrogant and rude behaviour of the group. This gives rise to a feeling that support by a pressure group is essential for survival, welfare and little flexing of muscles of indulgence in indiscipline; the price of allegiance and in disciplined acts, when called for, extracted by the pressure group seems a fair bargain.

- ***Non-teaching Employees***

The universities have a large number of unskilled, semiskilled and low skilled employees, with little motivation or facilities for improvement of skills. This fact, combined with the relatively fewer positions available at higher level and the leisurely work culture makes their productivity far below the capacity and leads to frustration and consequent indiscipline. The number of employees can be reduced, in a phased manner by (i) contracting out services (ii) training and (iii) modernization of equipment and procedures. The frustration can be avoided by a promotion policy based on seniority and skills, training programmes to acquire/improve skills must be made available. Such an approach will improve efficiency and lead to higher employee satisfaction without extra expenditure.

- ***Teachers***

The dissatisfaction of teachers arises mainly from lack of interest in and/or lack of facilities to carry out serious academic work; the society's perception of the importance of teachers, as illustrated by their relatively low importance also adds to their woes. Indifferent students and poor infrastructure also help to reduce interest in academic work.[1]

Maintenance of Campus Discipline

Campus indiscipline is a socio-political and psychological issue. Maintenance of discipline on the campus means dealing with the socio-political and psychological factors. It needs a double approach. On the one hand, measures to prevent the occurrence of indiscipline have to be taken and on the other hand actual incidence of indiscipline has to be suitably handled.

Prevention of indiscipline would mean checking the factors that are responsible for the breakdown of discipline. Several steps need to be taken in this direction. First of all, it is necessary to create and maintain an academic ethos that is conducive to the pursuit of higher learning. The responsibility for it lies mainly with the teachers and administrators. It is extremely difficult to maintain an academic atmosphere within our campuses unless the top administrators themselves are capable ad academically oriented. The same is true of the teachers. Unless the administrators and teachers are committed themselves, they cannot provide the students with an academic atmosphere on the campus that can serve as a powerful antidote to indiscipline.

Also, every educational institution should have an effective grievance redressal mechanism. Most cases of indiscipline on the campus are found to be reactions to grievances of the students that have not been properly or effectively handled. Not only students but even teachers need grievance redressal. Dissatisfied and frustrated teachers will not only be unable to prevent student indiscipline but also may provoke students into indiscipline. In the absence of suitable grievance redressal mechanisms, teachers themselves have started resorting to pressure group activity. This is increasingly undermining their credibility as academics and reducing their ability to prevent student indiscipline. Thus, setting up effective grievance redressal mechanisms for both students and teachers seems to be an important step towards preventing incidence of indiscipline on the campus.

Another preventive action that can be taken is controlling politicization. It is high time that an effective method is devised to check the political influence on the campus. Unless the administrators and teachers themselves are willing to resist politicization, we cannot expect severing the political links in the case of the students. It is a difficult task when the head of the institution himself is a political appointee and much worse, a person whose credentials as an academician or educationist are poor.

Many of the psychological factors responsible for the occurrence of indiscipline can be prevented through good counselling services. Some of the institutions of higher education do have such a service.

But they do not seem to be professionally managed. Students of higher education are in a critical state of their life and are likely to face various types of emotional stresses and strains. They need to be trained in life skills and emotional intelligence so that they can positively face the challenges of life. They need to be properly guided and helped so that they do not react to these tensions in the form of indiscipline.

At the macro-level, prevention of student indiscipline would mean, dealing with the socio-economic and political factors that promote campus indiscipline. It also means revamping of the economic system so as to reduce unemployment, cleansing the political system to control politicization, and restructuring the social system in order to institutionalize, appropriate values that will counter anti-social tendencies like corruption, untouchability, injustice and exploitation. While one can hope for social change outside the educational system that will contribute to the creation of an atmosphere conducive to campus discipline, teachers and educational administrators should do their part in ensuring discipline.[2]

Approach to alleviation

- ***Students***

Activities of criminal nature cannot in general be controlled by the university management, but can be best curbed by the police, with the cooperation of the university authorities. However, action by police may lead to student unrest, unless executed with fairness, tact and care to see that the innocent are not harassed.

The university should reorganize itself as a student friendly system. The academic programmes, evaluation system, rules, regulation procedures and facilities should be redesigned to have maximum value for the students. The academic programmes should be made relevant and of high quality, implying challenge and hard work on the part of the students; the seriousness, concern and courtesy of teachers and employees, the facilities for co-curricular/sports activities, the nature of evaluation system and counselling service should be commensurate with the commitment to provide best total education, suitable for maximising employability and ability to contribute meaningfully to knowledge and society on the part of the graduating students. If this basic issue of educational reforms is seriously addressed there is little hope of alleviation of student indiscipline.

Another important aspect of alleviating student unrest is an effective credible mechanism by which grievances of students are heard on an individual and/or collective basis and genuine sincere efforts made to alleviate these in a time bound expeditious manner. In case no action can be taken, the reasons should be explained. The university administration should make all out efforts to establish credibility sincerity and efficiency in student relations. Meaningful communication with students should be pursued continuously.

The significant achievements of students in studies, sports and co-curricular activities should be publicly recognized to motivate the channelization of student energy in these fields. The academic programmes should also be made challenging and relevant, particularly for employment, requiring serious efforts on the part of the student. Special efforts should be made to have students take up sports and/or co-curricular activities. This will leave little time for students to engage in undesirable activities.

Use of unfair means in the examination is a major area of student indiscipline. The anti-copying ordinance by U.P. Government which made copying a cognizable offence was highly effective in reducing the menace of unfair means in examinations, to a very large extent. Threat or use of force by or on behalf of an examinee should be made a cognizable offence; wherever such a provision exists effective machinery for implementation should be evolved. Use of multiple question papers and problem oriented thought provoking questions for which answers are not available can also discourage copying. A challenging academic programme and rational evaluation system, which makes the use of unfair means redundant is the best way to combat this menace. Good coordination with and optimum use of police is a necessary condition for combating the menace of the use of unfair means in examinations under the present conditions. The strategy should be achievement of the objectives by show rather than use of force because the latter leads to agitations and more indiscipline.

As indicated earlier the hostels represent centres of student indiscipline in the system. In addition to providing a de facto immunity to students and others engaged in illegal activities, the hostels also harbour a number of unauthorized residents. Needless to say that the hostels can be cleared of unauthorized persons, and maintained in that state by closely coordinated action by the university authorities and the police and continuous vigilance.

Meaningful participation of students in university management should be encouraged. In academics the class committees including nominated/elected, conduct and networking with the outside world of the academic programme. Students can contribute effectively to leadership and management in co-curricular activities, sports, NCC etc. and interaction with the world outside the university. Representatives from different activities can form a student body for coordination and items of a general nature. Advisors from faculty may oversee the activities making sure that the financial discipline is maintained.

The present style of students union with directly elected key office bearers has outlived its usefulness and needs drastic reform, so that students organize different activities and participate in university management, without any deviation from normal behaviour.

- ***Non-teaching Employees***

Genuine efforts to help, continuous communication, an effective, expeditious and transparent grievance redressal system and non-interference in trade union activities, should be important aspects of non-teaching employee policy of the university; however "no work no pay" should also be a constituent of this policy.

- ***Teachers***

The university should strive to provide an atmosphere which encourages academic work and recognizes excellence of individual teachers. Regular assessment of work and discussion of the assessment with the teachers should be a regular feature. An Ethics Committee consisting of teachers may be formed to strengthen ethical practices and consider violation of ethical norms. Obvious acts of indiscipline like unauthorized absence from classes, private tuitions etc. should be dealt by disciplinary action under rules. Other undesirable behaviour can also be countered by action under rules.

The main difficulty in combating indiscipline is the fact that various bodies of the university have abundant representation of teachers and tend to take a lenient view of any lapse on the part of teachers and others. Hence there is a need to create an atmosphere of scholarship and associated behaviour so that indiscipline acquires a horrible rather than overlook able quality.

There is an urgent need to induce change in thinking about discipline and punishment. Sincere and deep understanding is required to think about the strategies so that these acts of indiscipline do not recur or recur with minimum. For teachers there are two paths viz. either to be popular or to be a good teacher. One has to choose priority. The fresh graduates or the new adults are for the first time being exposed to a college and a university life, also to the members of the opposite sex (especially boys and girls who have studied in only girls and boys schools respectively). They need to be trained and guided as to how to behave with the girls and how to maintain a positive relationship with opposite sex. It is the moral duty of the teachers especially to actively intervene and counsel the students in this aspect. We need to be in tune with the present times and accept the changes taking place around us. It is only then that we can help and guide our students and inspire them to follow the correct path. These new adults need to be trained in becoming tolerant.

Politics in University Campus: Boon or Bane

The death of Hyderabad University student Rohith Vemulain 2016 was extremely tragic. Five PhD students, Dontha Prasanth, Rohit Vemula, Vijay Kumar, Sheshaiah Chemudugunta and Velpula Sunkanna, all Dalits, were banned from entering hostels, the administration building and other common places in groups, and were restricted from participating in the Students' Union elections, following certain incidents that happened between ABVP and ASA on August 3, 2015.The decision to suspend these students was taken by an Executive Council, the highest body of the University, without conducting a proper inquiry. The ASA compares this to the prevalent practice of upper castes ostracising a Dalit household from villages. The suspension was also against the then Vice-Chancellor's order that revoked the earlier suspension demanding a fresh inquiry on the incidents that happened on August 3 and 4.[3]

His suicide letter was poignant, deep and thought-provoking. In it, he showed glimpses of being the writer that he aspired to be and it is sad that such a future for him will never be. This also brings us to a larger question of why all our students face so much of political pressure in the first place instead of focusing on education, actual philosophical debate, their dreams and their unfolding futures.

There has been a recent spurt in incidences of violence, strikes and protest movements in our educational institutions like Jawaharlal Nehru University, Film and Television Institute of India, Hyderabad University etc. albeit for different reasons. Regardless of how genuine or not-so-genuine their reasons are, the situation raises some very important questions. Do we need politics in our institutions? If it is allowed, how much politicisation is desirable, for a line has to be drawn somewhere? And more importantly, what kind of politics do we want?

The apathetic response, the action or inaction by those in charge, to such protests raises even more serious questions. Do our institutions of higher learning enjoy the requisite autonomy, so that they reflect the democratic ideals that our nation espouses? What factors affect this autonomy? How can we guarantee this cherished autonomy of our institutions given the realities of their administration? And why do only a handful of our institutions enjoy a monopoly of producing political leaders? These questions are not only important for universities but for the nation.

Autonomy and accountability are the two sides of the same coin. These are complementary to each other. Autonomy without accountability may lead to anarchy. Accountability without autonomy may turn into regimentation. A balance or a "trade off" between the two is necessary- which may depend on the prevailing social climate and which in any case has to evolve through experience. Thus, where autonomy means independence in thought and action at different levels in a university, it enjoins upon it a greater responsibility in a democratic set up to act with greater restraint so as to be open to social audit, public scrutiny and a more sustainable participative management. Every organ of the university should work towards the common goal of the university suppressing its individual pursuit of objectives, which may sometimes conflict with the overall objectives of the system. Everyone should realize that the time has come for deep introspection about the accountability to the society.

To understand the need for politics in our institutions, the realities of society we live in need to be understood. Politics today, whether desirable or not, has become all pervasive in nature all around the world, varying only in terms of degree. It has become so widespread that there exists no social institution that is not affected by politics or is devoid of internal politics. Our economic development viz. industries, corporates, social welfare schemes, health, education, infrastructure development is all guided by political policies and practices. Political patronage determines the benefits the people of a particular religious community enjoy. Politics controls to some extent the creativity of our artists.

If politics is so deeply entrenched in our system, how can universities be an exception? If the goal of a university is not myopically defined to train students only in a particular discipline, but is to prepare students for unforeseen and unimagined things that life has to offer, then politics is very important, as a part and parcel of college activities, for the overall development of an individual's personality and character because character building is the first step to nation building. Also, politics is needed in institutions not only because it is present everywhere but also to produce better leaders who can sacrifice their life for their country. Since college politics has direct links with national and state level politics, it becomes a good launching pad for new faces that otherwise would not have had a chance to enter the political arena. Therefore, student politics can institutionalise the merit-based search for future leaders.

The need is to introduce positive and healthy politics in our big and small institutions so that best talents can come out and can be trained to become our future leaders. The answer to violent activities based on political pressures lies not only in disallowing any form of politics in campuses but also changing the kind of politics and the mind-set that we practice.

Political theorists argue that democratic politics is not only about the ritual of elections, political canvassing etc. but refers to the dialectical environment of debate, discussion, dialogue and dissent in a peaceful setting. The intention is not to demolish opposing ideas but recognising the right of others to have differing thoughts or ideologies than yours. The same should be the case for politics in the universities. The need of the hour is that the leaders of tomorrow must rise to the occasion and devise new and innovative ways of dissenting and protesting through their writings, movies, plays, songs, using the power of social media and the internet without disrupting the academic discipline of the institution. Also, they must not deprive others of their right to study in a peaceful environment.

Any and every university can put up a structure for participation of students in running the University for Example in IIT's. It's a good place to meet like- minded people and learn and grow together. The campus community forms a close knit group and students get friends for their lifetime. The campus, the people and this life make them a stronger and confident person. There is a "Students' Gymkhana"(composed almost entirely of students in executive positions). Anyone interested in opening a club of his interest can get approval from this unit and can progress further.

Mahatma Gandhi said, "A nation's culture resides in the hearts and in the soul of its people." The Cultural Council of the Students' Gymkhana organizes a plethora of activities spanning over the whole year. With a calendar punctuated by scores of workshops and classes over the year, including the summers, the Council provides the students profuse platforms to pursue various cultural genres, train themselves, perform on stage or just appreciate various cultural arts. The students are also given a chance to hone their skills and compete with other prolific colleges in intercollegiate cultural festivals. The council gives ample opportunities to the students to cement them into the cultural scene at IIT's through events like fresher's night, impressions, galaxy (Inter-Hall Championship) and other club events. Such activities will help in building constructive politics which is must. Through these activities elections can take place; these people can elect their secretary and everywhere there can a faculty advisor.

We have too many people crying foul over appointments of V-Cs, heads of departments or institutes due to the political leanings of the person concerned. It is required that the appointment process be made more transparent and should involve all stakeholders, even the student community and civil society. As many universities are still in the formative stage, the vice chancellors have to display unusual qualities of leadership. Academic traditions have to be built up, sustained and raised in order to inspire all sections of the university community. This is essential to ward off petty problems on the campus. These are bound to be minimized if the Vice Chancellor himself sets an example of work culture. Foresight, clarity, quick action, honest and impartial attitude are needed in taking decisions.[4]

The institutional autonomy gets diluted if the governing board is constituted on political considerations rather than based on the demands of competent governance. The role of the governing board is to provide broad policy guidelines, strategic directions, and help the head (say, the director) of the institution to raise funds. The board will also ensure academic autonomy and freedom of decision-making to the faculty and protect it. It is perhaps desirable that the governing board and the faculty, rather than the government, should have a greater say in appointing the director to ensure autonomy. The real autonomy lies with the authority and freedom of academic staff ensuring the efficient and effective functioning of the institution.

As far as the successful implementation of the complete process is concerned to bring transparency and discipline in the campus we should be open to all ideas and suggestions, the matter should be sorted out by a screening committee and the disciplinary body (Proctor) should tell what should be done and will take approvals accordingly. In emergency situations he should be able to act on his own.

There is a widespread concern in the educational community about the proposed private university Act since all writers have voiced their fear of loss of autonomy. Fixing fees and appointing/removing Vice Chancellors brings in a suspicion of being run by remote controls. It is rather unfortunate that a wide spread debate amongst intellectuals and professors has not taken place. The education system can lose innovation and vitality unless there is widespread support for a proper Act by all political parties.

The Crux

The problem of campus indiscipline is essentially linked to the decline of academic spirit. Various socio-economic and political factors have contributed to the deterioration of this ethos and have functioned as stimulants to student indiscipline. We are at a stage when both preventive measures and corrective action need to be taken in order to maintain discipline. The initiative especially as regards preventive measures are concerned, should emerge from within the campus itself. Teachers and administrators of educational institutions have to play the leading role in maintaining campus discipline.

Maintenance of campus discipline is to be achieved through both preventive measures and disciplinary action against indiscipline. The teachers and the educational administrators should constantly endeavour to provide an atmosphere on the campus conducive to academic work and to maintain effective grievance redressal mechanisms. Deviant behaviour should not be tolerated. Both these measures viz. preventive and disciplinary are necessary and one cannot be effective without the other.[5]

References

1. Srivastava K. & M.S. Sodha (1997). *Indiscipline in Universities*, University News, 35 (15), pp. 1-4.
2. Aikara Jacob (1994). Campus Discipline: Restraints and Controls. In M.V. Mathur, Ramesh K. Arora and Meena Sogani (Editors), *Indian University System: Revitalization and Reform* , Wiley Eastern Limited, New Delhi, pp. 246-249.
3. https://www.indiatoday.in/fyi/story/what-happened-at-hyderbad-central-university-that-led-to-rohit-vemula-suicide-304365-2016-01-18
4. Rastogi R.P. (1994). Role of a Vice-Chancellor. In M.V. Mathur, Ramesh K. Aroraand Meena Sogani (Editors), *Indian University System: Revitalization and Reform,* Wiley Eastern Limited, New Delhi, pp. 113-122.
5. https://www.youthkiawaaz.com/2016/02/need-for-student-politics/

Reflection - 9

Emerging Role of Higher Education for Human and Social Development

Nature of Indian Higher Education

Education is the most critical input in shaping human destinies. The social opportunity for developing human capability is the key towards a more equitable and efficient society. The natural potential of any person requires educational inputs to provide a framework for individual development. The goal of education is to make human beings who improve the quality of life of the society they live in. While basic education provides a framework for skill development, it is higher education that provides the edge towards the ability of individuals and nations to compete and survive in the global world. Higher education is also a form of social development as ultimately it is the improvement in the lives of the people that determines the success of such efforts. Education, in order to be meaningful to society, has to promote a culture of participation, sharing and brotherhood. Education based on narrow selfish interests and pursuits often become self-defeating as it deprives the human beings of the value system. It is in this larger context of higher education as a factor for social development that we need to look at the Indian system.

Universities are the key institutions in generation and dissemination of knowledge. These institutions work in the public interest and constitute the backbone of economic and social development. Many commissions headed by eminent educationists of post-independence era have reviewed the growth and development of education in India. The Radhakrishnan commission (1948-50) visualized a system of higher education, whose objective was to produce good human beings.

The Kothari Commission's (1964-66) five-point charter of higher education aimed at generation of new knowledge, leadership, competence building, equality and social justice, still remains as a beacon of guiding principles of our educational policies. Higher education is responsible for training future professionals to occupy strategic positions in the society and the work force. Consequently, the universities play a fundamental and decisive role in enhancing knowledge, values and skills in the students. Despite this, the government and the public often view a university as mere generator of knowledge and training center for leaders and elite workers of the future. This attitude is detrimental to the role of universities in nurturing desirable culture in the society. Education and the culture developed through education have not met the challenges for sustained national and human development. Prof. Kothari rightly pointed out *"In a science based world, education and research are crucial to the entire development process of a country, its welfare, progress and security."*

The role of higher education in today's world is immense, complex, and vital. A wide range of challenges and possibilities are emerging, with political, economic and social implications. Perhaps the most significant challenges are associated with shifting perspectives on knowledge itself, which strongly influence the role and the responsibility of the university in the context of the society. The role of higher education institutions has changed over time from preservers of culturally revered forms of knowledge, through producers of skilled labour associated with a manpower planning approach, to the more recent perception as the agent of social change and development.

The most explicit role, allocated to higher education is the production of highly skilled labour and research workers to meet perceived economic needs. However, during periods of social transformation, associated with far-reaching changes in the economy, universities can play an important role in helping to build new institutions of civil society, in encouraging and facilitating new cultural values, and in training and socializing members of the new social elites. In a general sense education may be viewed as a life long process of growth and as an activity, which brings about changes in the social environment. The process of human development too, invariably means change, a change for the betterment of society. Hence, continuous efforts for human resource welfare characterize both education and development at the conceptual level.

Impact of Higher Education on Society and Culture

Two major considerations in planning higher education at the national level are the development of human resource for the economy and the impact on social stratification. The most easily recognized impact of higher education on society is connected with the graduation of students, at various levels and their subsequent participation in productive work. This is usually assessed in terms of the number of graduates and the corresponding acquisition to the knowledge pool. Indeed, this work force expects to enter as an important element in the planning of higher education. The reciprocal nature of the impact of higher education is evident. "Does the outflow of graduates correspond to the demands of the society in quantity and quality?" is a key question. The demand is usually determined by the number and job descriptions of the available job positions; it does not take into account the impact of the employers.

There is no perfect fit between the knowledge, gained by the graduates, their career preferences, and the employment needs of the society. Oversupply, shortage and mismatches in the educational content, may be partly overcome by suitable planning, adaptation or emphasis on empowerment for learning. However, the extent to which the qualifications and knowledge of the graduates from educational institutions should conform to the expectations of the society is a central issue. Education should not only be commensurate with the demands of presently available positions but should develop a learning ability, which makes a person adapt to changing needs and technology. Higher education can be an independent force in the society, bringing branches of knowledge into action other than those foreseen by the planners, businesses or political bodies in the past and present.

An explicit or implicit philosophy, concerning the fit between the outflow of graduates and the expressed needs of employers, is an important element in the planning of higher education. The political decisions of higher education planning are related to potential student numbers, to the location of educational opportunities, to buildings and equipment, and to financial frames rather than to the content and the organization of studies. However, the institutional framework created by political decisions, such as the principles for governance of the institutions, the planning of resources for research, the connection between higher education and working life, and so on, also affects the quality of the education.

The impact of higher education on the social fabric and culture is in general indirect long term one rather than immediate and extends over long periods of time. The specialization of knowledge is often regarded as an important contribution of higher education to modern society. Indeed, the continuing specialization of research in virtually all fields of science is fundamental to the structure of higher education. A graduate is trained only to look at the world from a specialized viewpoint for example of a computer scientist, an economist or an orthopaedic surgeon. But behind the division of labor- horizontally into an increasing number of specialties, and vertically into the separation of planning and leadership from implementation and routine are the social forces that enhance concentration of power and the formation of large scale organizations. Such trends in the society influence the formation of higher education institutions; large universities may function as models for the organization of knowledge in industry, hospitals etc.

Social responsibility of Higher Education

As centers of production and dissemination of knowledge and training, higher education institutions are well positioned to link the local and the global. This gives them considerable access to and influence over change processes in many societies; this enhances their potential to contribute to human and social development. They are therefore called upon to play a fundamental role in building the society.

Higher education is responsible for training the professionals, who in the course of their careers attain positions of great responsibility and power in the society and the labour market. Throughout the world the decisions of professionals, trained in the universities, can make an important contribution to the way that life develops on this planet. This decision-making can take place through approaches that are either positive or negative for the global progress of humankind and societies, in both developed and developing countries. Higher education, therefore, plays a decisive and fundamental role in terms of the teaching content, values and skills for prospective leaders and the elite.

The implications of the main trends in information and knowledge for education are enormous. From a *knowledge society* perspective, education will play a vital role in the sharing, application and creation of knowledge in a globalizing world. Higher education and universities in particular will, it is claimed, “fuel the driving forces of the transformation towards a global knowledge society” and have “a certain capacity to steer and eventually to correct the direction of trends within globalization”.

Globalization offers many major opportunities to the universities but also raises serious problems for the future by questioning the feasibility of the guiding values of higher education. The changes brought about by globalization are so pronounced that we now need to reconsider the relationship between higher education and society. Resources are being channeled into education and knowledge creation like never before, so much so, that we are defacto embarking on the creation of the knowledge society. There is a general appreciation of the fact that higher education provides the competencies that are required in different spheres of human activity, ranging from management, agriculture, business, industry, health, communications, arts and culture. As higher education institutions are the institutions responsible for creating and spreading knowledge, and thus contributing to solutions to global problems, the relationship between scientific research and political decision-making needs to be explored and analyzed. The role of science and technology to serve political decision-making for the collective well-being is a neglected subject that higher education should also address.

The World Bank document *Higher Education: The Lessons of Experience* (World Bank, 1994) allocates a low priority to higher education in its scheme of funding, yet admits: "*Higher education is of paramount importance for economic and social development. Institutions for higher education have the main responsibility for equipping individuals with the advanced knowledge and skills required for positions of responsibility in government, business and the professions.*" Thus, there is a need to arrive at some basics, which should be incorporated in our educational programs for ushering a desirable change in human and social development during the current millennium.

Where is development heading?

An overarching trend of present times is globalization, associated with the move towards a global economy, and political transition from national to international organizations. These changes have resulted in an increasing debate on the notion of development. Hotly debated over decades, and with origins in the field of biology, development has been equated by many with global economic growth, which would result in all the peoples of the world achieving economic parity with those living in the "developed" nations. Over time, "human development" has, however, acquired more complex meanings. The UNDP states:

> *Human development is about much more than the rise or fall of national incomes. It is about creating an environment in which people can develop their full potential and lead productive, creative lives in accord with their needs and interests. People are the real wealth of nations. Development is thus about expanding the choices people have to lead lives that they value. And it is thus about much more than economic growth, which is only a means - if a very important one - of enlarging people's choices....Fundamental to enlarging these choices is building human capabilities —the range of things that people can do or be in life. The most basic capabilities for human development are to lead long and healthy lives, to be knowledgeable, to have access to the resources needed for a decent standard of living and to be able to participate in the life of the community. Without these, many choices are simply not available,*

and many opportunities in life remain inaccessible (UNDP website, accessed 2006).

Voices are now being raised, some from within the universities themselves, warning that the models that have guided development on earth over the last century are by now obsolete. The need to rethink the current development paradigm and collective social values is getting more and more acute. The incorporation of new contents that can equip people with new tools more suited to the context in which they carry out their professions is unavoidable. Individual and collective responsibility in professional decision-making within the new global ethical paradigms will be a subject of serious thought in the immediate future. Higher-education policies can no longer ignore such an urgent demand.

If universities and higher education institutions are to support processes of human development and positive social change, in addition to continuing their role as generators of knowledge, there is a need to go beyond the narrow concepts of knowledge. There is a need for a sincere engagement between universities and society, which should extend far beyond national boundaries. The nature of such an engagement demands debates and intensive deliberations, based on real examples, practices and experiences. There is also a need to understand the role that the universities will play in this engagement, particularly in the ways that they engage with citizens – both individuals and collectives. This may be achieved in part by the forging of new relationships by universities and the emergence of networks that ensure continued relevance of higher education "for the promotion of a healthy social and political climate within a country along with economic and cultural development".

Universities can therefore, play an active role in debate and public and private action by generating responses to the transformations in societies from an innovative perspective. This is a crucial moment to revisit the role of higher education, starting with the present and the past, to project visions for the future.

Higher Education for Human and Social Development

Higher education is neither solely for pumping knowledge into young heads nor is it just a place for secluded scholars in monk-like solitude. Higher education is a meeting place of generations, of cultures and of social classes. This is one of the rare societal institutions where rich and poor, adolescent and mature, knowledgeable (professor) and naive (student) and old and young meet and pursue an intellectual life together. This is where a culture of knowledge and intellect gets germinated, formulated and shared; this is where one learns first hand, of other cultures, social classes, and new perspectives.

Higher education can play a key role in human and social development on the international scale; this role has specific characteristics and different approaches in different regions. If higher education is channeled appropriately, it can address major world issues such as poverty, abuse and denial of human rights, strengthening of democracy, conflict resolution, peace building, environmental concerns, and the preservation and extension of human rights. Universities and other higher education institutions are in a position to examine these complex problems and to arrive at innovative solutions. Working in collaboration with international networks the universities must develop a prospective vision of the different scenarios, of alternative solutions to ongoing problems, of the political dimensions of these problems, and of the capacity to move forward in an uncertain future.

It is important that the university system consciously enhance its relevance. Certainly, the university system should be relevant to the society in which it functions. This relevance can be judged by its sensitivity to and concern for the society and its capability to respond to its needs, resulting in a better insight into the problems and significant contribution to the search for solutions. One of the major goals of the university system is to multiply knowledge, skills and other aspects of human potential in the country. The university system is unique in performing this function. While other systems use knowledge and skills, the university system multiplies and generates these for the sake of various institutions and organizations. Multiplication of talents through excellent education contributes to all the three aspects viz. research, teaching and application.

Whereas an individual is trained to acquire skills and arts of writing and reading at basic levels in higher educational institutions, skills are refined to groom professionals. The need is to produce young men and women as job givers rather than job seekers. This requires a thrust in diverting actions and skills of humans towards entrepreneurship and leadership not only politically but also economically and socially. This should be possible by matching our resources to our needs. Therefore, we have to make our students acquire skills and knowledge, which shall enable them to be active partners in our social system and bring about corresponding development of mind. There is a need to incorporate partnership in higher education, where parents, teachers, students, administrators and the political system enter into face-to-face interaction to develop the capacities of our students.

The university need not be a mere degree or diploma giving factory but has to integrate knowledge and work to produce degree and diploma holders who are able to address the real problems faced by the masses. They have to be trained in appropriate skills to utilize waste bye products and untapped resources. This would bring an economic revolution. These institutions in the distance mode could disseminate awareness among women on house keeping, food preservation etc and vocational courses. Utilizing university teachers, a system of workshops and seminars, training and awareness programs could be launched by the universities, as is the case with Directorate of Extension Education in agricultural universities. Future educational policies have to incorporate a mechanism for spiritual training, so that spiritual power is invoked by our students to pursue peace, justice, brotherhood, equality and dignity.

Social Problems and the role of Higher Education

In a developing society like India, there is no doubt that universities and institutions imparting higher education can play a significant role in anticipating and solving social problems. Despite the prestigious and privileged place assigned to institutions of higher education, few initiatives in tackling social and political problems have been undertaken. Although, access to higher education has rapidly increased in the last fifty years, its benefit is limited to only specific social classes or groups. Evidence shows that some communities and groups are under-represented in higher education. It is due to this fact that higher education is viewed as elitist and as a vehicle to perpetuate social inequities. University-society interface can help in tackling social problems and lead to social development.

- ***Creating new knowledge***

Universities are in fact a microcosm of the society; the elements of diversity and democracy are common to both. In view of this reality, Universities can no longer be content only with imparting knowledge. Universities have the potential to draw from the stock of knowledge and pave the way to provide solutions for social, cultural and economic development. Considering their vast resources the Universities are in an excellent position to adapt knowledge to solve specific problems and challenges.

Related to this aspect is the knowledge construction process which relates to the extent to which teachers help students to understand, investigate and determine how the implicit cultural assumptions, frames of reference, perspectives and biases within a discipline influence the ways in which knowledge is constructed. It is important for students to understand how knowledge is constructed in all disciplines. Students need to understand even in Sciences how cultural assumptions, perspectives and frames of reference influence the questions that researchers ask and formulate (Banks, 92).

- ***Content integration***

The teachers can use examples and content from a variety of cultures and groups to illustrate key concepts, principles, generalizations and theories in their subject area or discipline. This fusion, however, should be logical and not contrived. More opportunities exist for the integration of ethnic and cultural content in some subject areas than in others. In the social sciences, the Languages, Arts, Music and Home Economics there are frequent and ample opportunities for teachers to use a variety of ethnic and cultural content to illustrate concepts, themes and principles.

- ***Equity pedagogy***

An equity pedagogy exists when the teachers modify their teaching in ways that will facilitate the academic achievement of students from diverse cultural, ethnic and gender groups. Research indicates that low income students as a group, tend to differ from middle class students in some important characteristics related to motivation (Lefcourt, 1976). Low-income students tend to be external in their motivational orientation, which means that they tend to attribute their success or failure to outside forces or individuals and not to their own efforts. Middle-income students tend to be internal in their orientations. These characteristics of low income and middle class students is just one example of how teaching can be modified to increase the academic achievement of students from diverse social class, cultural and gender groups. Other strategies include the use of cooperative teaching strategies.

- ***Civilizing the human mind***

Education has a fundamental significance in development and progress of human society. It is the channel for creating awareness and appreciation of diversity, widening the understanding of varying groups of people, intensifying sensibilities of cultures and beliefs and inculcating the spirit of enquiry and questioning of accepted truths. In other words, education has the capacity to free the human mind from ignorance and false sense of self- preservation.

- ***An empowering institutional culture***

Another important aspect involves restructuring the culture and organization of the institutes so that students from diverse ethnic, language, religion and gender groups will experience equality. This variable must be examined and addressed by the teachers, Head/V.C./ Principal and support staff. It involves an examination of the latent and manifest culture and organization to determine the extent to which it fosters or hinders educational equity.

- ***Creating opportunities for livelihood and growth***

An important condition of democratization in higher education is the provision for equal opportunities of access for all classes and groups. University education has found popularity as the ladder to achieve status and career satisfaction. Inspite of massive expansion, higher education has failed to equalize educational opportunities and increase employability after completion of studies. There is a need to expand the capacity of institutions in the fields related to natural sciences, social development and technology.

- ***Nation development***

The concept of democratization should extend to include a commitment by universities in regard to their own responsibilities towards nation development. This role would include national and social integration with emphasis on needs of low income and marginalized groups.

- ***Research and interdisciplinary approach for problem solving***

It is apparent that the research potential of higher education in various aspects of integrated development can be used to help provide solutions for development. The capability of higher education institutions to undertake the process of analysis and reflection and to promote a spirit of critical inquiry needs to be utilized to the maximum.

Future Strategies: Actions and Plans

Effectiveness of the university system can be defined in terms of four main aspects of the functioning of the university system viz. autonomy, creativity, collaboration and self-renewal. The autonomy of both the individuals and the university itself can facilitate the achievement of its goals. Although providing autonomy does not ensure effectiveness, it is a necessary condition, particularly for a competent faculty. Similarly, creativity characterizes effectiveness. Creativity is the use of innovative ways of moving towards the goal rather than sticking to ways, which were decided some time. Collaboration amongst the various persons and constituents in the system is equally important. Finally, self-renewal, the ability for dynamical change with experience for the better is also an important characteristic. All the four characteristics put together can be called 'organizational health'.

There is agreement that future strategies and actions should focus on the design of pathways and methods that will guide higher education towards achieving organizational health and a balance between economic development, on the one hand, and human and social development, on the other. There is consensus that sustainable development cannot be achieved without human and social development. Such development can be achieved-

- by creating a meritocratic system of admission to higher education programs for individuals from all regions and backgrounds;
- by reinforcing the critical function of higher education and corresponding academic freedom;
- by developing higher education systems that are adapted to the needs of society;
- by strengthening the contribution of higher education to other levels of the education system; through diversification of higher education models; based on research on sustainable development;
- by ensuring gender equality in higher education system and by strengthening the profile of higher education as a public service and a public good ;
- by harnessing the growing globalization of higher education as a tool for consolidating international cooperation; and
- by maintaining a culture of peace
- by value education
- by emphasizing on practical and applied aspects

Universities should become more innovative and responsive "to the needs of a globally competitive knowledge economy and to the changing labour market requirements for advanced human capital" (World Bank, 2002). Curriculum has to be understood as both process and outcome and should be oriented towards providing well-equipped workforce for a globalizing economic world. Policy goals of efficiency, effectiveness, responsiveness and competition may work against the potential of higher education to contribute to human and social development Curriculum has to be derived through a process of dialogue around the ideologies, philosophies and epistemologies of knowledge and learning. Two key directions for curriculum that support learning for human and social development are bridging between existing disciplines and moving towards a transversal, interdisciplinary curriculum. Curriculum change has to be inclusive, just, democratic, oriented towards citizenship, and based on transformative and participatory processes.

The quest of higher education for human development would require a focused attention on the needs of the poor students who make it to the university system. While revision of fees in the university system has become necessary on account of the growing demand and reduced financial grants for education, such measures have necessarily to be accompanied by an efficient, timely and appropriate system of scholarships, freeships and loans for the needy students.

The three-point program

In the context of higher education, an important event at international level took place in the form of world conference on higher education held at Paris from 5 to 9 October, 1998. As a result of world conference, UNESCO (1998) issued a set of recommendations, *World Declaration on Higher Education*, which has two distinct parts. In the first part, the UNESCO has envisioned higher education in terms of roles and functions that it should play in socio-cultural and economic development of nations *"as a fundamental pillar of human rights, democracy, sustainable development and peace."* In the second part, recommendations are made for concrete and specific steps that need to be taken at national and international levels for change and development of higher education and overall enhancement of its quality and relevance. Therefore, all the four pillars of the system of education i.e. students, faculty, infrastructure and policies, need to be taken in consideration.

According to **Philip G. Altbach,** director of the Center for International Higher Education, Boston College, universities throughout the world are increasingly being asked to maintain their key functions in the face of budget restrictions, which leads to a deterioration in the level of service offered. It seems that there is neither the time nor the money that would enable universities to consider new approaches to education or social involvement. In this climate, universities with extensive research programs have been most adversely affected by the need to find new sources of funding, and have found themselves forced to modify their operational structures considerably.

The government and the public often view universities simply as generators of wealth and training centers for key professionals of the future, but can this attitude produce tangible benefits for higher education and for society as a whole? Universities have been forced to sacrifice aspects of their essential role as centers that foment intellectual and cultural development, social analysis and comment. At the same time, they have become increasingly tied to the practical needs of society, dictated by governments and markets (this is particularly true in the case of private institutions). Altbach warns that "societies which ignore the multiple purposes and functions of universities will be very weak, since universities are driving forces behind the creation of wealth and knowledge but must also work towards humanistic and cultural objectives and individual needs".

For this purpose, a three-point program of qualitative improvement with a focus on manpower development, quantitative expansion for the removal of barriers to equitable access in higher education and promoting research and development activities is the need of the hour. Experts believe that universities have the following functions:

- Universities are responsible for the education of a sizable proportion of the workforce.
- University curricula across the world have traditionally been based on specialized knowledge in specific disciplines and have not included general type of learning. The role of this type of education is currently being debated; it has already been incorporated into university curricula in some disciplines.
- Preserving and disseminating knowledge.
- Intellectual centers for knowledge creation.
- Universities are now national and international institutions due to the increasing number of partnerships and the general trend towards globalization.
- Driving forces behind economic development.
- Instrument of social mobility.

We have to emphasize inculcation and dissemination of values. Values are dynamic undergoing creation, modification and rejection all the time. Since time immemorial it has been recognized that education is necessarily a process of inculcating values to help the learner lead a good life that is satisfying to the individual in accordance with the cherished values and ideals of the society. Philosophers, spiritual leaders and educationists have emphasized the role of education for character development, bringing out the latent potentialities and inherent qualities and developing integrated personality for the well-being of the individual and the society at large, highlighting the need for value orientation of education.

Despite its several thousand years old value-based cultural tradition, India is also subject to massive erosion of values. The rapid degeneration of human values in the Indian context has posed a big challenge before higher education. It is a recognized fact that modern education and training have failed to produce men and leaders of character and integrity who can make India attain its past glory. Worldwide there is a cry for going back to basic values so that the strength to deal with the complexity of modern living is developed. There is a need of a comprehensive programme of value education which can enable students to meet new situations in today's world as well as in future.

Preparing for life with a scientific temper is more essential than preparing for examination. For a country to grow meaningfully and in a sustainable way, the university systems and colleges have to become centers of propagation of values.

Looking back on the developments in the higher education sector over the last five decades, it is heartening to note that a number of institutions have obtained global excellence. The challenge is to make the number of such institutions grow, as ultimately the challenge of excellence and the challenge of equity have to go hand in hand. Human development is always universal and not individual; to this extent, the pursuit of knowledge has to become much more a social rather than an individual goal. In making human development a reality, partnership with the non-governmental sector has to be built in order that all the resources available to the country viz. human, financial and material are fully put to use for promoting excellence and equity. The modern times require greater focus on quality in higher education institutions in order to meet the challenges of the global economy. Change in attitude and a strengthening of higher education systems, are vital for achieving sustained human development. While the challenges may appear discouraging, the results can be achieved provided the entire society is involved in this process and shows commitment.

Conclusion

Change in attitude and a strengthening of higher education systems, are vital for achieving sustained human development. While the challenges may appear daunting, we can achieve the results provided we involve the entire society in this process and infuse commitment. At the present moment the universities seem to be utopian, but they do provide ideals to strive for. Higher education in the 21st century promises to be not only demanding but also refreshingly different. Imparted under the all-pervading influence of the communication technology revolution it has to be student-centered, committed to the concept of lifelong learning, responsive to the needs of society, increasingly privately financed, and influenced by the market forces. It has to be international in character placing emphasis on quality, with partnerships and networks being important.

In the early part of the 21st century life will be influenced not only by the 'knowledge society' but also by the 'stakeholder society' and the 'market society'. The universities, while creating and disseminating knowledge, also need to cater to the interests of its various stakeholders (students, parents, faculty, government, society-at-large), and to market demands. The pursuit of higher education has to be need-based rather than greed-based and for doing so, we need to evoke the philosophical framework that has been available in this great country. The pursuit of knowledge is a pursuit of self-realization. When looked at in this framework, higher education indeed becomes an instrument for human development.

References

Specific References

1. *Report of the University Education Commission* (*1948-49*), 1949, Ministry of Education, Government of India, New Delhi.
2. *Report of the Education Commission (1964-68): Education and National Development*, 1966, Ministry of Education, Government of India, New Delhi.

3. https://www.theguardian.com/higher-education-network/2018/jan/25/too-many-graduates-are-mismatched-to-their-jobs-whats-going-wrong
4. UNESCO 2005, *Towards Knowledge Societies*, UNESCO Publishing, Paris: UNESCO.
5. World Bank, *Higher Education: The Lessons of Experience*, 1994, The World Bank: Washington, D.C.
6. http://hdr.undp.org/en/content/what-human-development
7. Banks, J., 'Multicultural Education: Approach Dimension and Developments', In *Mudgal (Eds.): Multicultural,* 1998.
8. http://www.egyankosh.ac.in/bitstream/123456789/8445/1/Unit-9.pdf
9. UNESCO, 1998, *Higher Education in the Twenty-first Century: Vision and Action*, UNESCO, Paris.
10. Forest, J.F., and Altbach, P.G (Ed.), 2006, International Handbook of Higher Education Part 1: Global Themes *and Contemporary Challenges,* Springer, Netherlands.

General References

1. Brennan J. and Y. Lebeau, 2002, *The role of universities in the transformation of societies. An international research project*, paper presented at the CHER 15th Annual Conference, 2002 5-7 Vienna, Austria.
2. *Higher Education: Its Context and Linkages*, IGNOU, 2003, MES-101, pp. 18-21.
3. Kaw, M.K., 2000, 'Valedictory Address'. In *Higher Education for Human Development,* K. B. Powar (ed.), Association of Indian Universities, New Delhi, pp. ix-xi.
4. New challenges and emerging roles for human and social development, *The 3rd GUNI report onHigher Education in the World* presented at the 4th International Barcelona Conference on Higher Education, held at UPC between 31 March and 2 April 2008.
5. Soni, R., 2007, Intellectuals' Expectations from a University: An Exploratory Study, Ph.D. Thesis, Department of Education, University of Lucknow, Lucknow.
6. The International Encyclopedia of Education: Research and Studies. Vol. 4 F-H. Editors-in-chief: Torsten Husen, Paragon Press, Oxford. pp. 2220-2223.
7. Venkateswaran, S., 2000, 'Presidential Address'. In *Higher Education for Human Development,* K. B. Powar (ed.), Association of Indian Universities, New Delhi, pp. iii-vii.
8. Van Damme, D., 2002, *Outlooks for the International Higher Education Community in Constructing the Global Knowledge Society.* Paper presented at the First Global Forum on International Quality Assurance, Accreditation

and the Recognition of Qualifications in Higher Education. UNESCO, Paris. 17-18 October 2002.

9. Varma, M., Sodha, M.S., and Soni, R., 2007, *Teachers' Expectations from their own University: A case study of University of Lucknow*, Journal of Indian Education, XXXIII (2), NCERT, New Delhi.
10. Soni, R., 2012. *Higher Education: India and Abroad* Vol. 1, Atlantic Publishers, New Delhi.

Index

B

C

O

P

Q

R

S

T

U

V